Brainstorming Activities

Middle School

by Ann Fisher

Published by McGraw-Hill
an imprint of

Author: Ann Fisher

Children's Publishing

Published by McGraw-Hill
An imprint of McGraw-Hill Children's Publishing
Copyright © 2004 McGraw-Hill Children's Publishing

All Rights Reserved • Printed in the United States of America

Limited Reproduction Permission: Permission to duplicate these materials is limited to the person for whom they are purchased. Reproduction for an entire school or school district is unlawful and strictly prohibited.

Send all inquiries to:
McGraw-Hill Children's Publishing
3195 Wilson Drive NW
Grand Rapids, Michigan 49544

Brainstorming Activities—middle school
ISBN: 0-7696-3398-6

1 2 3 4 5 6 7 8 9 MAL 09 08 07 06 05 04

The McGraw-Hill Companies

Table of Contents

Brainstorming Introduction 4

1-Minute Brainstorming Activities

Guidelines for One-Minute Brainstorming Activities 6

Activities 1–90 7

2-Minute Brainstorming Activities

Guidelines for Two-Minute Brainstorming Activities 37

Activities 1–60 38

5-Minute Brainstorming Activities

Guidelines for Five-Minute Brainstorming Activities 68

Activities 1–35 69

Brainstorming Introduction

Brainstorming Benefits

Brainstorming in the classroom enhances the learning process. Thinking of a new way to connect ideas, finding a different way to use something, or substituting one thing for another are all elements of brainstorming. It helps students warm up at the beginning of the day or the class period. It allows them to hear answers from peers that they may not have considered themselves. It often produces excellent solutions to problems. Brainstorming activities

- encourage free-flowing and flexible thinking
- cultivate good listening skills
- enhance communication skills
- expand reasoning ability
- sharpen problem-solving and critical-thinking skills
- increase vocabulary
- push students to draw on their diverse experiences and backgrounds to come up with creative solutions
- facilitate collaboration
- create fun

In the beginning, students tend to give common, practical, and obvious answers, but they will gradually become better at improvising creative solutions. Think of brainstorming as a mental aerobic exercise. The more the mind is exercised, the better it works. To get your students' brainstorming "muscles" in shape, start with the short and simple activities in the one-minute section. Then gradually strengthen their mental muscles by advancing to some of the two-minute and then the five-minute questions.

Brainstorming Activities in This Book

The activities in this book encourage creative thinking in language arts, mathematics, social studies, and science. They provide graduated opportunities for your students to think creatively. The progressively longer time limits and complexity of the activities require progressively deeper thought and analysis.

The one- and two-minute activities can be completed orally. The one-minute activities introduce students to the concept of brainstorming and to participating in verbal response and exchange. The two-minute activities get students to begin connecting ideas in brainstorming and to consider common words and objects in new ways.

The five-minute activities require more complex solutions. They include a student recording sheet for responses, along with a teacher page, for each activity.

Brainstorming Basics for Students

Successful brainstorming can only take place in an environment free of judgment and criticism. The following rules will encourage such an atmosphere in your classroom.

1. **Use your imagination!**
2. **Don't worry if your idea is good or not.**
3. **All ideas are acceptable in brainstorming. There is no criticism, judgment, or grading.**
4. **Quantity counts! The more ideas the better.**
5. **Keep your ideas brief. Give details later.**
6. **Your idea can piggyback or build on someone else's. Combine ideas to make a new one.**
7. **Think quickly!**

Brainstorming Basics for the Teacher

Creative thinking has to be nurtured. Encourage your students to think creatively every day. Try to fit in one brainstorming activity daily, when it best fits your classroom routine—first thing in the morning when students come into class, as they line up for lunch, just before they get ready to go home, or during a transition between subjects.

Specific guidelines for using the exercises appear at the beginning of each section. Brainstorming can be done by individuals, in pairs, or in small groups. In general, follow the one-minute, two-minute, and five-minute time limits closely. They force students to use their time efficiently. Use a stopwatch, a timer, or a student clock watcher. But if a session is going particularly well and ideas are still flowing, by all means, feel free to continue! Extend time limits. Omit parts of any activity. Adapt the activities to meet the needs of your students.

Sample solutions for most activities are included. However, your students will probably come up with very creative answers of their own. The sample answers provided are not intended to be a complete list of possible solutions. Accept all reasonable answers, but always ask for clarification if an idea has not been clearly communicated. If you like, add some of your students' answers in the blanks provided in this book. You can use them in brainstorming sessions with future groups of students.

Brainstorming Uses

While verbal responses alone are perfectly suitable to a brainstorming session, you may wish to have students record even the one- and two-minute sessions in a notebook. Brainstorming generates lists and ideas students can use in writing essays, reports, stories, journal entries, explorations in science, or in creating math problems for others to solve. Use the activities to introduce a new unit of study, as extensions to study, and as preparation for brainstorming competitions. Adopt what works best for your situation.

Discussion after brainstorming is highly recommended. The amount of time spent is up to you, the teacher—one minute or ten, depending on how you wish to use the brainstorming activity. Encouraging students to discuss how they came up with a response or discussing the more unusual responses may help others think more creatively in the next session.

Most importantly, have fun!

Guidelines for 1-Minute Brainstorming Activities

The one-minute activities provide a comfortable introduction to brainstorming. The questions encourage brief answers—and lots of them. These are suggested guidelines for using the one-minute activities on pages 7–36.

1. First decide how to group students. For such brief activities, students may work alone or in pairs.

2. Be sure each student has a blank sheet of paper and a sharpened pencil before beginning.

3. Read the question clearly. Repeat it. Ask students if they understand it. If not, give a brief explanation.

4. Tell students when to begin, and then time them for one minute. You may wish to announce when 30 or 45 seconds have passed.

5. At the end of one minute, ask students to stop writing.

6. Instruct students to read over their responses and mark two or three of their favorites.

7. Ask for volunteers to share their favorite answers with the entire class. The teacher should write these on the board for everyone to see.

8. Be aware that humor is an important element in brainstorming. The process often leads to funny answers—good!

9. After several volunteers give their answers, ask if other students have different responses from those offered.

10. Be careful not to reject answers. Instead, you may wish to comment on those answers that are particularly clever, creative, or amusing.

11. Mention some of the sample responses included in this book if they are significantly different from your students' answers. *Please note: The sample answers provided are not intended to be a complete list of possible solutions.* If you like, add some of your students' answers in the blank spaces in this book. You can use them in brainstorming sessions with future groups of students.

12. After each brainstorming activity, you may want students to make notes in a notebook or on a log sheet. Students can record 1) the question or activity, 2) their own responses, and 3) classmates' responses they liked best. They can also leave space to record other answers that come to mind later.

13. Consider transferring lists written on the board to large sheets of paper that you can hang in the room and referred to later in other activities. For example, the responses to activity 64, on page 28, could serve as material for a creative writing assignment.

What things have stripes?

Sample Solutions: bar codes, zebras, candy canes, jail uniforms, officers' trousers, neckties, socks, parking lots, pinstripe suits, the track at a track-and-field competition, divided highway, Navajo woven blanket, throw rug, wallpaper

_____
_____
_____

Think of a new name for a paper clip. Do not use the words "paper" or "clip" in the new name.

Sample Solutions: document clasp, letter holder, memo grip, bent-wire gadget for holding printed sheets, metallic binder, document attacher, metal fastener, sheet slip, wood-fiber binder

_____
_____
_____

What kinds of wheels can you list?

Sample Solutions: bicycle wheels, car and truck wheels, the wheels on the bus, cartwheels, spinning wheel, Wheel of Fortune, wheel on a merry-go-round, "lazy Susan" wheel, steering wheel, "wheeler-dealer," Wheeling (city in West Virginia), wheelbarrow

_____
_____
_____

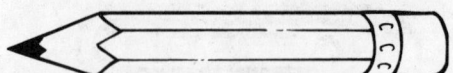

4 You have a very special piece of fabric. It is rectangular. What could it be?

Sample Solutions: a flag, a hand-embroidered heirloom, your mother's wedding veil, a designer belt, an authentic Elvis neck scarf, a long, narrow guitar strap that belonged to a famous musician, the outer layer of a beloved childhood pillow

_____

_____

_____

5 List reasons why trying to write with a pencil may not work.

Sample Solutions: It needs to be sharpened; the lead is broken; the lead is missing; the room is dark and you can't see if it is writing; you're trying to write on black paper; the paper you're writing on is coated with a substance that makes the lead immediately disappear.

_____

_____

_____

6 List anything you might study in school that begins with *a*.

Sample Solutions: art, arithmetic, algebra, anatomy, accounting, Asia, Africa, Arctic Circle, addition, autumn leaves, astronomy, adjectives and adverbs, animals, agriculture

_____

_____

_____

Name things that you blow.

Sample Solutions: a kiss, your nose, a bubble, a balloon, birthday candles, your cool, a test, flute, clarinet, harmonica, saxophone, trombone, trumpet, tuba, piccolo, French horn, bassoon, oboe, whistle, comb, kazoo

_____
_____
_____

List musical instruments that are not played with the mouth.

Sample Solutions: Drums, guitar, cymbals, xylophone, chimes, harp, violin, cello, viola, tambourine, maracas, triangle, wood block, musical spoons, musical saw

_____
_____
_____

List places named after US presidents.

Sample Solutions: Washington, D.C.; George Washington Bridge; Jefferson City, Missouri; Lincoln, Nebraska; Ronald Reagan Washington National Airport; Lyndon B. Johnson Space Center; JFK International Airport; Richard Nixon Library; Van Buren County, Michigan (and other states as well), Gerald R. Ford Presidential Museum; Monrovia, Liberia; and many possible schools and/or streets in your community

_____
_____
_____

10 What kinds of hands can you list?

Sample Solutions: right hand, left hand, hired hand, shorthand, handshake, hand-out, helping hand, handyman, handle, clock hand, hand of cards in a card game

_____
_____
_____

11 You have a huge box of uncooked macaroni. Besides cooking it and eating it, what else can you do with the macaroni?

Sample Solutions: string it on thread to make a necklace; glue it on a piece of construction paper in the shapes of faces, animals, cars, etc.; use it to fill a beanbag; put it in a jar with a tight-fitting lid to make a musical shaker; put it in a decorative glass canister

_____
_____
_____

12 What things can you name that are salty?

Sample Solutions: popcorn, peanuts, potato chips, pretzels, the ocean, tears, ham, pickles, herring, sardines, bacon, caviar, someone's speech

_____
_____
_____

A friend is having a birthday. You want to honor your friend in a creative way. Other than giving a gift, what can you do?

Sample Solutions: Call a radio station and ask to have the birthday announced and/or ask to have a special song played in your friend's honor. Send an electronic greeting card. Make your own card. Put a big Happy Birthday sign in her or his front yard. Ask all of your friends to call and wish her or him a happy birthday.

___

Tell how a tennis racquet is like a football.

Sample Solutions: both are used in a sport, both contain string, both are held in the hand, both may be brown

___

Name as many different kinds of mail (*m-a-i-l*) as you can.

Sample Solutions: junk mail, snail mail, e-mail, spam, first class, third class, priority mail, airmail, overnight mail, registered mail, bulk rate mail, packages, postcards, magazines, newspapers, letters, chain mail

16 **Finish this word: news** _____

Sample Solutions: newspaper, newscast, *Newsweek* magazine, newsroom, newsworthy, newsprint, newsstand, newsletter, newsperson, news flash

17 **Write down many different ways to show the number 9.**

Sample Solutions: 9, nine, XIX, ||||| | | | |, 10 – 1, 17 – 8, 4 + 5, 6 + 3, 3 x 3, 81 ÷ 9, 27 ÷ 3, $\frac{27}{3}$

18 **How many things can you list that are used in the home to prepare food?**

Sample Solutions: stove, microwave, food processor, refrigerator, mixer, toaster, can opener, juicer, blender, bread machine, colander, bowls, spoons, timer, cutting board, knives, chopper, grater, cooks, cookbooks

How many words (no names) can you name that begin with *h* and end with *y*?

Sample Solutions: hay, hey, happy, happily, handy, handily, honey, hairy, honestly, healthy, hobby, holy, holly, highway, hierarchy, hospitality, huckleberry, hasty, hastily, hearty, heartily, hanky

___

___

___

What kind of licenses can you list?

Sample Solutions: driver's license, marriage license, pilot's license, dog license, hunting license, chauffeur's license, medical license, poetic license

___

___

___

Name things with horns.

Sample Solutions: cars, trucks, buses, deer, antelope, moose, rhinoceros, bull, unicorn, elk, sheep, orchestras

___

___

___

22 **Make a list of things with keys.**

Sample Solutions: piano, computer keyboard, typewriter, organ, accordion, locks, maps, calculator, jailer, monkeys, turkeys, donkeys

_____
_____
_____

23 **Name as many sports as you can name that are played with a ball.**

Sample Solutions: baseball, softball, basketball, football, soccer, tennis, ping pong, croquet, bowling, golf, volleyball, bocce, cricket, racquetball, dodge ball

_____
_____
_____

24 **Name as many sports as you can that are played without a ball.**

Sample Solutions: track and field, bicycling, badminton, shuffleboard, darts, hockey, car racing, judo, karate, bobsledding, harness racing, swimming, rowing, figure skating, in-line skating, slalom

_____
_____
_____

Make a list of things you frequently wash.

Sample Solutions: your hands, your hair, your car, the dishes, your face, the laundry, the floor, the dog, fruit, vegetables

_____
_____
_____

What might you see on a playground?

Sample Solutions: slide, teeter-totter, merry-go-round, swings, rings, gliders, sand, gravel, asphalt, monkey bars, happy children, parents, teachers, litter, grass, bucket and shovel, sandbox, toy cars, balls, bikes, scooters, baby strollers, park benches

_____
_____
_____

List words or phrases that begin with *life (l-i-f-e)*.

Sample Solutions: lifelong, life insurance, life jacket, life boat, life flight, Lifesavers™, lifetime, life-size, lifeguard, life expectancy, lifeblood, lifelike, life-giving, life span, lifetime, life-or-death, life-and-death

_____
_____
_____

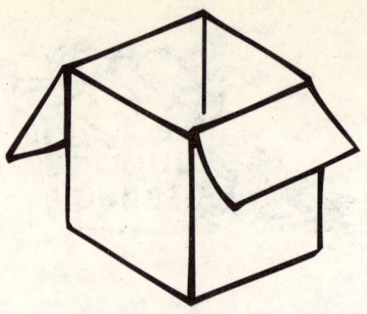

28 **List as many boxes as you can.**

Sample Solutions: shoe box, cardboard box, shirt box, pill box, mailbox, safety deposit box, music box, jewelry box, storage box, toy box, window box, cereal box, boxer shorts, boxer (dog), box car, box lunch, box seat, box spring, boxing (sport), box office, box social, Boxing Day, boxboard

_____

_____

_____

29 **You observe your younger brother or sister sitting on the sofa with hands over eyes. What might you infer?**

Sample Solutions: Something very scary is on TV. The sun is shining brightly through the window and the child is shielding her eyes from it. The child just splashed something in his eyes, and they are burning. If the child is very, very young, she might think by covering her eyes so that she can't see you, she is "hiding" so that you cannot see her.

_____

_____

_____

30 **A large amount of water found in nature might be called a pond, a river, or _____.**

Sample Solutions: an ocean, a sea, a lake, a stream, a creek, a bay, a bayou, an estuary, a gulf, an iceberg, a waterfall, a lagoon, a swamp, a glacier, a geyser

_____

_____

List as many modes of transportation as you can.

Sample Solutions: automobile, SUV, bus, truck, tractor, train, subway, jet, plane, helicopter, jeep, boat, ship, canoe, submarine, raft, bicycle, motorcycle, unicycle, tricycle, moped, snowmobile, ATV, space shuttle, rocket, blimp, hovercraft, glider, skis, skateboard, scooter

_____
_____
_____

Another word for *happy* is _____.

Sample Solutions: joyful, glad, pleased, excited, content, delighted, gleeful, cheerful, pleasant, fortunate, enthusiastic

_____
_____
_____

A window fan is running in your bedroom, pulling in air with a strong smell. What might be the source of the fragrance?

Sample Solutions: a flowering bush outside your window, a fruit orchard in blossom, a skunk, someone standing outside your room who is wearing strong perfume, insecticide that has just been sprayed to kill mosquitoes, bug-repellent candles, someone's incense from a nearby house, exhaust fumes from a car or truck

_____
_____
_____

34 **List words or phrases that begin with *head*.**

Sample Solutions: headache, headlight, headphone, headpiece, headline, heading, headstrong, headstand, headquarters, headlock, headhunter, head honcho, head-over-heels, headless horseman, head waiter, headway, head-to-head, headlamp, headfirst, headband, headmaster or headmistress

___

35 **Name things that are black.**

Sample Solutions: nighttime, tires, asphalt, hearse, ink, Model T Ford, charcoal, licorice, shoe polish, construction paper, some clothes, text in most books, videotape

___

36 **I can keep only a few possessions. They must all fit in a shoe box. I will keep _____.**

Sample Solutions: letters from friends, baby pictures, pictures of my family, my cash, my favorite socks, jewelry, Bible or other special book, baseball card collection, bank book, special childhood toy, souvenirs, savings bonds, stock certificates, food, water

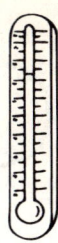

What things do we measure?

Sample Solutions: time, distance, length, weight, volume, temperature, barometric pressure, wind speed, blood pressure, heart rate, cholesterol levels, rainfall, wealth, intelligence

37

What things are we unable to measure with tools, equipment, or utensils?

Sample Solutions: happiness, friendship, grief, pain, contentment, peace of mind, success, fun, level of annoyance

38

Name as many kinds of nonfiction books as you can.

Sample Solutions: encyclopedia, dictionary, biography, autobiography, phone directory, atlas, thesaurus, almanac, owner's manual, cookbook

39

 **1 minute**

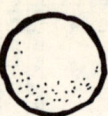

40 **If I lived on Mars, my pet peeves would be _____.**

Sample Solutions: cold temperatures, no atmosphere, little water, I would miss the people and places that I enjoy now, everything is red, my favorite foods, animals and plants

_____

_____

_____

41 **The ideal family car should be equipped with _____.**

Sample Solutions: a self-cleaning interior and exterior, a separate DVD/CD player for each family member, a soundproof panel between seats, a sauna, a chauffeur, a refrigerator

_____

_____

_____

42 **Describe the number 13 using as many different words or short phrases as possible. Do not use any number words.**

Sample Solutions: odd, unlucky, prime, unique, baker's dozen, a couple more than the players on a football team, all the fingers on your hands and some of the toes on a foot

_____

_____

_____

The ring was very magical indeed. No one had fully discovered its secret. It was so magical that when I put it on _____.

Sample Solutions: I went back in time. I instantly became my favorite hero. I knew the truth about the latest cover-up. I suddenly had special athletic abilities. I was never hungry again. I turned purple. I was a wise and beautiful/handsome queen/king.

43

_____
_____
_____

Name things that are polished.

Sample Solutions: fingernails, chrome on a car, shoes, furniture, brass instruments, trophies, floors, jewelry, silverware, cars, a speech, a resume, your vocabulary, your knowledge on a subject just before a test, a musical performance, the final draft of a writing assignment

44

_____
_____
_____

After school you ride the bus home. You observe a television crew outside your home. You know no one else in your family is home. What might you infer?

Sample Solutions: You just won a big sweepstakes, and the TV crew wants to catch you on film when you're told the good news. There's been a fire in your home, and it will be shown on the evening news. Something has happened at your neighbors' home and the television crew actually should be at their house. The President has chosen you to be her or his new advisor on teen topics.

45

_____
_____
_____

46 **Name things that are white.**

Sample Solutions: snow, marshmallows, clouds, wedding dress, milk, whipped cream, "White Christmas," correction fluid or tape, doctor's coat, handkerchief, paper, envelopes, shaving cream, foam on ocean waves, vanilla ice cream, salt, golf balls

_____
_____
_____

47 **Create some keys, other than letters and numbers, that should be on a computer keyboard.**

Sample Solutions: A+ science paper key, cold-drink key, potato-chip key, a teacher key that would give me all A's, a winning soccer team key, a homework key that would do it for you

_____
_____
_____

48 **Finish this word or phrase:** *left* _____

Sample Solutions: left field, left alone, left behind, left hand, left-handed, left of center, leftover, left wing, leftist, "Lefty," left turn

_____
_____
_____

What kinds of codes are there?

Sample Solutions: dress codes, secret codes, Morse code, ZIP codes, bar codes, Homeland Security codes (code blue, code green, code yellow, code orange, code red), code of ethics, code names, codebook, genetic code

---

Write down words that rhyme with *head*.

Sample Solutions: bread, bed, bled, dead, dread, fed, fled, led, lead, read, red, said, shed, sled, tread, wed, Ed, Fred, Jed, Ted, Ned

---

List people who wear uniforms.

Sample Solutions: people in the military, police officers, fire fighters, doctors, nurses, mail carriers, park rangers, waiters, beauticians, cooks, scouts, scout leaders, bus drivers, students in some private and public schools, astronauts, fast-food restaurant employees

---

52 **Finish this word or phrase: sand _____.**

Sample Solutions: sandpaper, sand castle, sandwich, sandstorm, sandbox, sandbar, sandbag, sandblast, sandstone, sandlot, sandal, sandalwood, sandbank, sand dollar, sander, sandman, sand lily, sandsoap, sandpit, sandpiper, sandpile, sand trap, sand table

_____
_____
_____

53 **What types of bread can you name?**

Sample Solutions: wheat, white, pita, rye, pumpernickel, Italian, garlic, French, egg, breadsticks, cornbread, hot dog buns, hamburger buns, muffins, rolls, toast, cheese, dilly, English muffins, bagels, cinnamon, raisin, pumpkin, apple, orange, pizza crust, fresh-baked bread

_____
_____
_____

54 **List things that are brown.**

Sample Solutions: dirt, wood, hair, eyes, shoes, socks, leather, coffee, tea, birthmark, brown sugar, root beer, cola, chocolate candy, hot chocolate, dead grass and plants, bamboo, brown bears, otters, beavers, freckles, cats, dogs, rabbits, squirrels

_____
_____
_____

The best things about being a major league baseball umpire would be _____.

Sample Solutions: You always make the final decision on a call. You have the final word. You are able to eject players and managers if they are rude. You are close to the action. You get a great view of the game. You get paid to go to baseball games, and you don't have to pay admission. You get to meet all the players.

_____
_____
_____

The worst things about being a baseball umpire would be _____.

Sample Solutions: No matter what call you make, someone is always upset: players, coaches, or fans. You may get booed by the crowd. You could get injured. You have to work sometimes in the rain or the hot sun. There is a lot of pressure to make the right call. If you make the wrong call and later realize it, your conscience could bother you.

_____
_____
_____

What things do people put lemon in or on?

Sample Solutions: ice tea, ice water, hot tea, fish, lemonade, lemon meringue pie, shrimp cocktail, soft drinks, furniture polish, countertop stains, their hair, a dog that's been skunked

_____
_____
_____

58 **You observe that all the students are carrying their lunches to school on a particular day. What inference might you draw?**

Sample Solutions: The entire school is going on a field trip. The cafeteria is closed for remodeling or cleaning. The cooks are on strike. No one likes the food on that day's menu. Every parent decided to save money by having students bring their own lunches instead of buying them at school.

_____

_____

_____

59 **List words or phrases that contain *heart—h-e-a-r-t*.**

Sample Solutions: heartache, heart attack, heart rate, heartbeat, heartbreak, heartburn, Purple Heart, heartfelt, heartless, heartrending, heart-to-heart talk, softhearted, hard-hearted, with all my heart, cross my heart, valentine heart, heart-shaped, heart-warming, heart surgery, fainthearted, heart-healthy diet

_____

_____

_____

60 **What aisles and departments might you find in a supermarket?**

Sample Solutions: meat, produce, frozen foods, dairy, canned goods, paper goods, health and beauty aids, deli, bakery, video, pharmacy, hardware, pets, automotive, furniture

_____

_____

_____

Think of as many occupations as you can that begin with *p*. Be creative.

Sample Solutions: pharmacist, pastor, printer, programmer, physician, plumber, photographer, psychologist, psychiatrist, paper hanger, pearl diver, podiatrist, peddler, pawnbroker, professor, planter, petty officer, perfume salesperson, pudding taster, pipe cleaner, puppy trainer, plum picker, pea picker, pear picker, Padres' pitcher, Peeping Tom, pied piper, pig farmer

61

Name things that keep or tell time.

Sample Solutions: wristwatch, clock, sun, sundial, pocket watch, computer, chiming clock, cuckoo clock, hourglass, work whistles, ship's bells, egg timer, time clock at work, radio announcer, VCR, microwave, TV on-screen display

62

List as many words of three or more letters as you can spell using only the letters in *computer*.

Sample Solutions: come, compute, cop, cope, core, cot, crop, cut, cute, cuter, cue, met, mop, mope, more, mote, mute, ore, our, out, outer, per, pet, pore, port, pot, pour, pout, prom, pure, put, romp, rope, rot, rote, route, rue, rum, rut, term, top, tore, tromp, tour, truce, true, trump

63

64 **List some things a skunk might say to a person just before it sprays its strong fragrance.**

Sample Solutions: "Okay, human, how do you like this?"
"Here's what you get for poking around my home!"
"Sorry, I just can't control it."
"Will this help you remember that I live here?"
"Have a whiff of this!"

____
____
____

65 **Give your best excuses (both reasonable and ridiculous) for not turning in your homework.**

Sample Solutions: The dog ate it. My little sister/brother tore it up. I lost it on the bus. We had a family emergency last night, and I wasn't able to complete it. You told us it wasn't due until tomorrow. I was busy doing an extra-credit project for you. My mother was terribly ill and needed a lot of help last night. I was terribly ill last night and wasn't able to work. I had extra chores last night because we are expecting the President to visit today. My grades are so much higher than my sister's/brother's that my dad asked me to let my grades slip a little to prevent sibling rivalry. I fell off my skateboard and had temporary amnesia. I had to watch World Series game seven because my dad was pitching for the Yankees. I put it over a little old lady in the rain, and she walked away with it.

____
____
____

66 **What things ring?**

Sample Solutions: telephones, church bells, timers, alarm clocks, chimes, ears, fire alarm, school bells, the truth, bell on a bicycle, an accurate horseshoe throw

____
____
____

An envelope is delivered to the palace under heavily armed guards. What could be inside it?

Sample Solutions: a top-secret message from a spy in another land reporting to the king and queen on an enemy's preparation for battle; the code that will help the queen decipher a message from her daughter who is being held by kidnappers; a cashier's check for a million dollars; the final answer from a beautiful young lady regarding the prince's marriage proposal; a valuable antique document of some sort, a knock-knock joke, a chess move, a bill from the caterer of the last banquet

67

What materials can you name that are used for making clothing?

Sample Solutions: cotton, denim, wool, silk, animal furs, suede, leather, polyester, corduroy, satin, velour, velvet, rayon, acrylic, leaves, grass

68

List New Year's resolutions that people sometimes make or should make.

Sample Solutions: lose weight, eat more healthful foods, exercise more, stop watching so much television, spend more time on homework, read more books, spend less money, stop smoking, spend more time with the family, spend less time online, learn how to use more features on the computer, learn how to cook more foods, write more often to friends

69

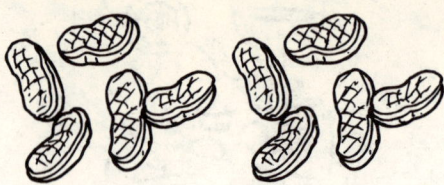

70 **The answer is $200. What is the question?**

Sample Solutions: If you earn $50 dollars a week for a month, how much will you earn in all? How much money do you get for passing Go in Monopoly®? If you start the month with $1000 and then spend $600 on rent and $200 on food, how much money will you have left? What is the price of 40 watermelons if each one costs $5? What will you charge to do my homework for me?

_____
_____
_____

71 **List many ways in which peanuts are used.**

Sample Solutions: peanut butter, candy bars, chocolate covered candy, cereal, roasted peanuts, mixed nuts, fudge, cookies, cakes, margarine, cooking oil, breads

_____
_____
_____

72 **What things are you likely to find on an executive's desk?**

Sample Solutions: telephone, intercom, stapler, tape, pencils, pens, newspaper, reading glasses, pads of paper, reports, computer, correction fluid, paper clips, radio, pencil sharpener, letter holder, framed picture, paperweight, name plate, appointment book, phone directory, clock, flowers, in box and out box, employee evaluations, candy dish, calculator

_____
_____
_____

What new flavors can you invent for toothpaste that might appeal to a lot of people?

Sample Solutions: chocolate, cappuccino, strawberry, lemon, lime, cherry, cinnamon, root beer, cola, orange, watermelon, sour apple, caramel, butterscotch, vanilla, hazelnut, chicken, beef

_____
_____
_____

What new flavors can you invent for toothpaste that might not appeal to a lot of people?

Sample Solutions: onion, garlic, corn, cucumbers, zucchini, pumpkin, avocado, tomato, popcorn, salt and vinegar, tea, cardboard, macaroni, chili, salsa, celery, sage, Limburger, dill pickle, old tennis shoe, sour milk

_____
_____
_____

Think of many ways you can reuse an old telephone book.

Sample Solutions: Use a thick one as a booster seat at the dinner table for a young child. Use a heavy one to flatten papers, art projects, etc. Rip out a few pages at a time to use when starting a fire in the fire place. Bind several thick books together with duct tape, cover them with fabric, and then use as a footstool or door stop. Use the advertising sections to find ideas for advertising your own business. Use the residential listings to find interesting names to use for characters when writing stories.

_____
_____
_____

76 **When is a one-dollar bill better than a one-hundred-dollar bill?**

Sample Solutions: when the hundred is lost or stolen; when you want to buy an item that costs only a few cents and the cashier does not have change for the large bill; when you want to give a stranger some cash and you only have one bill in your wallet; when someone accuses you of stealing a hundred-dollar bill

___

77 **List things that come in pairs.**

Sample Solutions: shoes, socks, boots, slippers, gloves, mittens, feet, hands, eyes, ears, arms, legs, earrings, earmuffs, dice, eyeglasses, salt and pepper shakers, wedding rings, jeans, twins

___

78 **Think of the longest sensible sentence you can in which every word begins with the letter *m*.**

Sample Solutions:

My mother, Martha, makes marvelous, melting marmalade.

Many magnificent mangoes made Mark's mustang mysteriously merry.

Marvin's most melodious mandolin makes mellow music.

Michigan's marble manufacturers measure most mansions.

Most modern Martians make mixed melodies magically.

1 minute

For what reasons might someone want to keep a frog as a pet?

Sample Solutions: It's an unusual pet. It's easy to find. It's inexpensive. It's active and fun to watch. Frogs are not noisy or destructive. Someone might like warts. Someone might hope it would turn into a handsome prince.

79

What kinds of brushes can you name?

Sample Solutions: toothbrush, hair brush, paintbrush, make-up brush, wire brush, toilet bowl brush, lint brush for clothing, nail brush, vacuum cleaner brush, shoe brush, brush cut (crew cut), brushfire, brush with death, brush up (as to brush up on one's math skills), brushwood, brush fire

80

Finish this word or phrase: *house* _____.

Sample Solutions: housewife, househusband, housebroken, housefly, houseplants, house rule, house trailer, housetop, housecoat, houseguest, houseboat, houselights, house of cards, housekeeper, household, housewares, house sitter, housewarming, house party, House of Representatives, House of Commons, House of Lords, house and home

81

82 **What people work outdoors?**

Sample Solutions: farmers, police officers, fire fighters, construction workers, garbage collectors, gardeners, truck drivers, cab drivers, bus drivers, street repair workers, snow plowers, ranchers, swimming pool cleaners, pest control workers, telephone line crews, exterior house painters, roofers, park rangers, security officers, lawn maintenance workers, fruit growers and pickers, sheep herders, letter carriers

_____
_____
_____

83 **What places have flags?**

Sample Solutions: U.S. Capitol, schools, police stations, city halls, political conventions, military bases, post offices, sporting events, voting places, the United Nations, veterans' graves, circuses, amusement parks, people's cars, churches, courtrooms, state capitols, ships and boats, auto races

_____
_____
_____

84 **What kinds of teeth can you name?**

Sample Solutions: wisdom teeth, molars, baby teeth, permanent teeth, capped teeth, incisors, canines, bicuspids, eye teeth, false teeth, wooden teeth, saw teeth, teeth on a zipper, cogs on a cogwheel

_____
_____
_____

What foods are best when they are hot?

Sample Solutions: soups, pancakes, scrambled eggs, sausage, hamburgers, French fries, fried fish, macaroni and cheese, stew

_____
_____
_____

What kinds of bulbs can you name?

Sample Solutions: light bulbs, three-way bulbs, 40-watt, 75-watt, 100-watt, Christmas tree lights, spotlights, floodlight, heat lamps, infrared, flashlight, bug light, fluorescent, tulip, iris, gladiolus, onion

_____
_____
_____

List things that cut.

Sample Solutions: scissors, saw, knives, pizza cutter, cookie cutter, hatchet, axe, clippers, sword, sickle, scythe, lawn mower, mean words

_____
_____
_____

88 **What types of ovens are there?**

Sample Solutions: electric, microwave, gas, self-cleaning, pizza, convection, kiln, toaster, built-in, warming, the outdoors when it's very hot

___
___
___

89 **If a gallon of milk could talk, what would it say?**

Sample Solutions: Please put me back in the fridge so I don't sweat. I'm sooooo good for you. Please drink me before I go sour. I miss my cow! I can give you strong bones and teeth. I go best with chocolate chip cookies. Don't pollute me with that chocolate powder, please!

___
___
___

90 **Name as many types of chairs as you can.**

Sample Solutions: folding chair, recliner, rocking chair, high chair, baby chair, armchair, wheelchair, wing chair, lawn chair, beach chair, chairman, chairperson, chairwoman, chairlift, electric chair

___
___
___

Guidelines for 2-Minute Brainstorming Activities

The two-minute brainstorming activities are designed to encourage inventive thinking. The idea in each activity is to consider everyday words or objects in a different, creative way.

1. First decide how to group students. Students may work alone or in pairs.

2. Be sure each student has a blank sheet of paper and a sharpened pencil before you begin.

3. Read the question clearly. Repeat it. Ask students if they understand it. If not, give a brief explanation.

4. Tell students when to begin, and then time them for two minutes. Announce when one minute has passed.

5. At the end of two minutes, ask students to stop writing.

6. Instruct students to read over their responses and mark four or five of their favorites.

7. Ask volunteers to share their favorite answers with the class. The teacher should write these on the board for everyone to see.

8. Be aware that humor is an important element in brainstorming. Expect the process to often lead to funny answers—good!

9. After several volunteers give their answers, ask if other students have different responses from those that were given.

10. Be careful not to reject answers. Instead, you may wish to comment on those answers that are particularly clever, creative, or amusing.

11. Mention some of the sample responses given in this book if they are significantly different from your students' answers. *Please note: The sample answers provided are not intended to be a complete list of possible solutions.* Accept all reasonable answers, but always ask for clarification if an idea has not been clearly communicated. If you like, add some of your students' answers on the blank lines provided in this book. You can use them in brainstorming sessions with future groups of students.

12. During or after each brainstorming activity, you may want students to make notes in a notebook or on a log sheet. Students can record 1) the question or activity, 2) their own responses, and 3) classmates' responses they liked best. They can also leave space to record other answers that come to mind later.

13. Consider transferring lists written on the board to large sheets of paper that can be hung in the classroom and referred to in other activities. For example, some responses could serve as material for future creative writing assignments.

2 minutes

1 **List as many things as you can that are printed.**

Sample Solutions: invitations, business cards, menus, brochures, announcements, advertisements, bumper stickers, campaign posters, resumes, letterheads, newsletters, envelopes, a child's handmade greeting card

___

___

___

___

2 **The best things to get rid of are _____.**

Sample Solutions: old clothes that don't fit, broken toys, socks with holes, anger, a bad reputation, harmful relationships, laziness, bad habits, negative attitude, old newspapers, self centeredness, recyclable goods, sour milk, spoiled food, ugly, outdated wallpaper, moth-eaten wool blankets, flea-infested furniture

___

___

___

___

Think of as many ways as you can to recycle the cardboard tube from a roll of paper towels.

Sample Solutions: blow on it for a horn, roll scarves and bandanas around it so they won't wrinkle, roll special papers and tuck them inside the tube, roll it over wrinkled papers to smooth them, flyswatter, smokestack on a toy boat or a silo on a model farm, backscratcher

_____
_____
_____
_____

I wish there were computer shortcut keys for _____.

Sample Solutions: writing thank you notes to relatives, writing school reports, the computer to read my mind and delete all unnecessary documents on my hard drive, creating clever jokes, solving difficult math problems, filtering out stupid Web sites from my browser, stopping the blinking and flashing online ads.

_____
_____
_____
_____

5 **Make a list of things for which you need a set of instructions.**

Sample Solutions: computer software, assembling a model car, making cookies, operating any kind of machinery, craft project, installing a ceiling fan or any appliance, becoming a new parent, driving to a specific place in a new city, learning a new instrument, doing school work

___

___

___

___

6 **List some phrases or sentences that you might be taught to use on your first day of training as a telemarketer.**

Sample Solutions:

Are you the homeowner?

We're conducting a survey in your area . . .

We'd like to send you, free of charge . . .

We'll be in your area soon and we'd like to set up an appointment with you to . . .

Due to your excellent credit rating, we can offer to you . . .

___

___

___

___

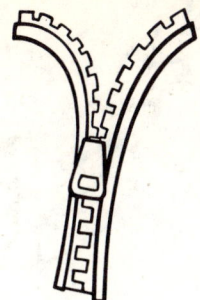

Name things that go up.

Sample Solutions: prices, the elevator, an escalator, a tent, a hot-air balloon, a helium balloon, a zipper, smoke, a kite, blood pressure, a fly ball, the cost of living, your age, the temperature on a summer day or in a crowded room, the tension in an important meeting, the excitement and noise at a concert

___

One-fourth of a mile is 1320 feet, or 440 yards. What other "one-fourths" can you show in at least two different ways?

Sample Solutions:

$\frac{1}{4}$ of an hour is 15 minutes or 900 seconds

$\frac{1}{4}$ of a year is 3 months or about 91 days

$\frac{1}{4}$ of a gallon is 1 quart, 2 pints, or 4 cups

$\frac{1}{4}$ of a dollar is a quarter, or 25 cents

9 If you take away the first letter in *braid*, you spell *raid*. If you take away the first letter in *preach* you spell *reach*. From what other words can you take away the first letter and spell a common word?

Sample Solutions: ahead, bladder, blow, cable, close, crush, crust, danger, drink, driver, ebony, fright, ghost, heave, hour, knew, mail, manger, nearly, nice, phone, plump, pirate, prim, ranger, relation, shall, slice, stable, stone, strip, tangle, their, thump, trifle, trim, valley, wash, weasel, weight, wring, yearn, yeast, zone

___

10 An *oxymoron* is something that cannot exist, such as warm ice. What other oxymorons can you think of?

Sample Solutions: a silent scream, an invisible freckle, cruel kindness, a wise fool, a stupid genius, a mellow fanatic, a huge speck, a lone competitor, unauthorized permission, mobile gridlock, a purple orange, plastic wood, a vague detail

___

Name things that you can catch.

Sample Solutions: ball, fly, fish, cold, train, bus, plan, mouse, "A Falling Star," running child, excitement, the chicken pox, a rash after touching poison ivy

_____
_____
_____
_____

More people could be enticed to become farmers if . . .

Sample Solutions: farmers didn't have to invest so much money in land and equipment, crops yielded higher profits, they weren't so dependent on the weather, farmers didn't have to get up so early, paparazzi followed a farmer's every move, farmers didn't have to deal with smelly animals, farmers got to dress up in tuxes and evening gowns and ride in limos, hens washed and sorted their own eggs, their parents said, "No way is a child of mine going to be a farmer!"

_____
_____
_____
_____

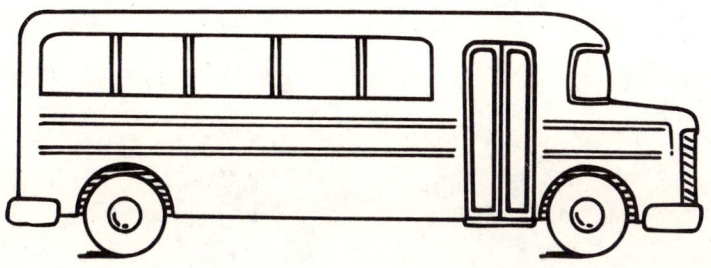

13 How many words of exactly 10 letters can you list? Do not use plurals.

Sample Solutions: applesauce, appreciate, background, comprehend, concession, conclusion, dictionary, eventually, government, jawbreaker, jeopardize, lumberjack, mayonnaise, monotonous, negotiator, pasteurize, separation, settlement, strawberry, tablecloth, tambourine, spellbound

___

14 You observe no one outside the school, no cars in the parking lot, and locked doors all around the building. You infer that there is no school today. What might be the reason?

Sample Solutions: It's Saturday. It's Sunday. It's a holiday. It's summer vacation. School was cancelled due to heavy snow or widespread illness. There is no electricity. There is no water. The school is not safe due to an environmental hazard. The school and/or community are under a terror threat. The teachers are on strike. Everyone was on a field trip yesterday and they were unable to get back. Aliens picked up everybody and locked up when they left.

What title could you give to a children's CD that contains songs about elephants?

Sample Solutions: "Elesongs"; "This Trunk's for You"; "An (Elephant) Ear for Music"; "Sing Along Songs for EleFans"; "Elephant Songs You'll Never Forget"; "Elephant Songs—No Jokes!" "Trunk Tunes"

15

_____
_____
_____
_____

How many words or phrases with the word *ice—i-c-e—*can you list?

Sample Solutions: ice cream, iceberg, ice cube, black ice, ice rink, ice skate, ice skating, ice hockey, ice water, ice pick, Ice Age, Iceland, icebreaker, icebox, dry ice, ice cap, ice-cold, ice dancing, ice milk, icehouse, cold as ice, ice fishing

16

_____
_____
_____
_____

2 minutes

17 **Suppose a small town held a celebration they called A-B-C Days. The *A-B-C* might mean Antiques, Blueberries, and Crafts. What else could it mean?**

Sample Solutions: Apple pie, Bean soup and Cherries; Always the Best City; Advertising Beats Complaining; Azaleas, Butterflies, and Critters; Antelope, Beef, and Coyotes; Agriculture's Bountiful Crops

_____
_____
_____
_____

18 **Name as many sources of light as you can.**

Sample Solutions: sun, star, candle, lightbulb, lamps, flashlight, neon signs, fireflies, moon, glow sticks, lighthouse, torch, lantern, street light, stop light, match, fire, headlight, floodlight, sunlamp, Bunsen burner

_____
_____
_____
_____

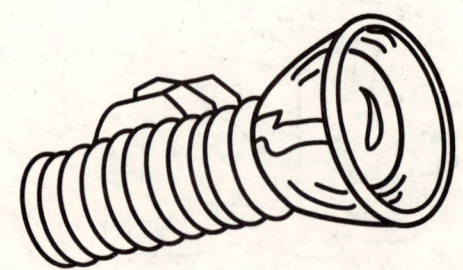

List all the possible factors that might affect the price of gasoline.

Sample Solutions: crude oil prices, supply of crude oil, war in oil-producing countries, taxes, transportation costs, advertising costs, demand for gasoline, refinery costs, cost of labor at gas stations, competing gas stations' prices, the Big Three automakers finally produce a car that runs on air, a chemist discovers a way to convert old textbooks to gasoline

___
___
___
___

List all the ways you can think of to prepare eggs.

Sample Solutions: fried, scrambled, hard-cooked, soft-cooked, poached, omelet, over-easy, sunny-side up, deviled eggs, pickled eggs, eggnog, Eggs Benedict, "hole in the bread," shirred, egg salad, with hash, egg foo yong, in pancakes, in meatloaf

___
___
___
___

21 **Make a list of adjectives that begin with *a*.**

Sample Solutions: abandoned, able, abrasive, abrupt, absent, acidic, acute, agreeable, alarming, alert, alive, all, allergic, allied, alphabetical, alternative, amazing, amicable, amiable, angelic, angry, animated, antiseptic, antisocial, anonymous, anxious, apologetic, apparent, appealing, apprehensive, apt, ardent, arduous, argumentative, artistic, astounding, athletic, atomic, automatic, awkward

_____
_____
_____
_____

22 **You wake up one morning and realize that everything in the entire world has turned green overnight. What things would seem the strangest to you in their new color?**

Sample Solutions: the sun, the sky, water, my skin, my teeth, all flower petals, the sidewalk, oranges and lemons, skunks, robins, snow, my teacher's hair, steak, milk, everything on television

_____
_____
_____
_____

One crying infant multiplied by twenty crying babies in a hospital nursery equals a wailing room. One worried mother multiplied by three teenage children equals a head of gray hair. What other things can you name and multiply?

Sample Solutions:

One eager concert fan multiplied by a thousand ticket holders equals a noisy, packed hall.

One dull wall multiplied by three gray rooms equals a gloomy castle.

One kind word multiplied by every child on the block equals a fun, safe neighborhood.

One small power outage multiplied by an entire power grid equals a major catastrophe.

_____

_____

_____

_____

How many *kings* do you know?

Sample Solutions: chess king, King George, King Henry, king of diamonds, clubs, hearts, or spades, kingdom, king-size, king cobra, kingfisher, king of the jungle, joking, looking, walking, talking, tracking, thanking, quacking, sinking, shaking, baking, thinking, breaking, kicking, clicking, soaking, Martin Luther King Jr.

_____

_____

_____

_____

25 A proverb is a short, wise saying such as, "A stitch in time saves nine." This means, of course, that taking care of a problem when it's small will save you much more work later. What other proverbs can you remember?

Sample Solutions:

A penny saved is a penny earned.

Every cloud has a silver lining.

Practice makes perfect.

Better safe than sorry.

Half a loaf is better than none.

Too many cooks spoil the broth.

Don't count your chickens before they hatch.

People who live in glass houses shouldn't throw stones.

Haste makes waste.

A penny saved is a penny earned.

Two heads are better than one.

Don't cry over spilt milk.

Where there's smoke there's fire.

Actions speak louder than words.

Better late than never.

Easy come, easy go.

_____

_____

_____

_____

26 **Make a list of things that you can pick.**

Sample Solutions: an ice cream flavor, a paint color, a mate, a winner, a china pattern, cotton, peaches, apples, cherries, strawberries, blueberries, peas, green beans, a peck of pickled peppers, a guitar string, a banjo, a scab, someone's brains

_____

_____

_____

_____

Start with *a*, *b*, *c*, and compose a sentence using words that begin with each letter of the alphabet in order. What's the longest sentence you can create? Here's one way to get started, as an example: Anna bakes cakes during . . . Or choose another place in the alphabet to start.

Sample Solutions:

Anna bakes cakes during Easter, following Greta's hors d'oeuvres.

Quentin respects Sally's talented undercover vigilance.

Healthy, imaginative, jolly kids love my new outlandish pickles.

Flipping griddlecakes helps improve Jesse Kay's lazy muscles.

_____

_____

_____

_____

Next start with *z*, *y*, *x*, or other consecutive letters, and make a sentence using the letters of the alphabet in reverse order.

Sample Solutions:

Zelda's yellow xylophone was very unusual to Stan.

Many lovely kittens jammed into Henry's gray fence.

Frankly, Edna's delicious cake baked automatically.

Perhaps Otto's new maid lacks keys.

_____

_____

_____

_____

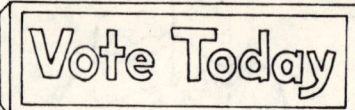

29 Voters were asked a question on the ballot to which they answered "yes" or "no." What was the question?

Sample Solutions: Do you approve the new school tax? Should Jane Doe be retained as the state supreme court judge? Are you in favor of this new law? Do you wish to recall your state's governor? Are you in favor of a new smoking ban? Do you wish to keep Daylight Savings Time? Should parents be allowed to set curfews?

_____
_____
_____
_____

30 The most important things that schools should teach middle school students are _____.

Sample Solutions: "Reading, writing and 'rithmetic"; how to pass the state's standardized tests; how to become better writers; how to read with more understanding; how to balance a checkbook; how to fill out a job application; all about our nation's history; how to get accepted into the best colleges; how to find a summer job; how our government works; how to stay healthy; the dangers of drugs, cigarettes, and alcohol

_____
_____
_____
_____

What things do people collect?

Sample Solutions: stamps, coins, garbage, donations, sports cards, souvenirs, junk, spoons, thimbles, menus, autographs, books, buttons, calendars, soda cans, advertising items, recipes, posters, comic books, dolls, hats, medals, models, pencils, pens, playing cards, jewelry, keys, trophies, stickers, stuffed animals, insects, rocks, seashells

___

List games children play that you don't have to buy.

Sample Solutions: tic-tac-toe; hangman; tag; duck, duck, goose; hide and seek; house; red rover; Mother may I; kick the can; ring-around-the-rosy; London Bridge; fruit basket upset; I spy; hopscotch; leapfrog; rock, paper, scissors; red light, green light; doctor; Simon says

___

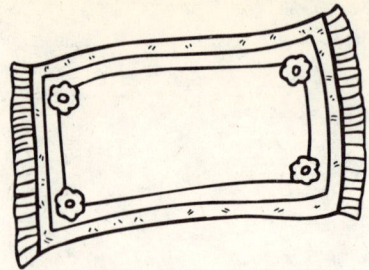

33 **Name as many reasons as you can why people might want to have a rug in their homes. Then name as many reasons as you can why people might not want one.**

Sample Solutions: Reasons for: to make a room quieter, to add color, to make the floor softer for children to play on, to make the floor warmer on bare feet, because a rug was given to them as a gift

Sample Solutions: Reasons against: because of the expense; because a carpet traps more dust than a bare floor, so someone allergic to dust might not want a rug; because pets can damage a rug; because food spills are hard to clean from a rug; because some people track in a lot of dirt, oil, grease, or paint from their work

_____
_____
_____

34 **List occupations that begin with the letter *s*.**

Sample Solutions: sailor, salesperson, sanitation employee, saxophonist, school-bus driver, school teacher, scorekeeper, sculptor, seaman, seamstress, secretary, serviceman and servicewoman, sewer worker, shepherd, shoemaker, shoe salesperson, singer, snow mover, soldier, sound technician, sportswriter, stage manager, station master, stock broker, store manager, street sweeper, student, superintendent, surgeon, surveyor, switchboard operator

_____
_____
_____
_____

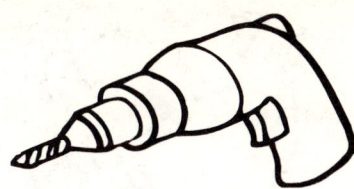

Tell where you might see the words *use caution*.

Sample Solutions: on a medication bottle, on a sign on a beach, when driving through a construction zone, when going down a flight of stairs, where falling rocks are possible when driving on a mountain road, on equipment such as power saws and drills, on a hair dryer or curling iron, on signs near power lines

---

Name as many words as you can that can be anagrammed to form another four-letter word. Here are two examples: tale—late, rate—tear. Note that some combinations of four letters may spell more than two words.

Sample Solutions:

same—seam, mesa	tame—team, mate, meat	fear—fare
heat—hate	cola—coal	care—race, acre
slab—labs	busy—buys	came—mace
colt—clot	coin—icon	disk—skid
diet—edit, tide, tied	east—teas, seat	file—life
free—reef	gasp—gaps	legs—gels
dial—laid	west—stew	thin—hint
chin—inch	lamp—palm	stop—pots, post
mean—name, amen		

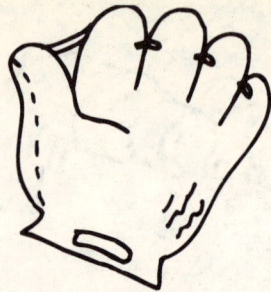

37 *Arthropods* are invertebrate animals (lacking a spinal column) that have hard outer coverings (exoskeleton) and jointed legs. Arthropods include insects, arachnids, and crustaceans. In two minutes, name as many arthropods as you can.

Sample Solutions:

insects: mosquito, fly, ant, bee, flea, louse, beetle, lady bug, grasshopper, cicada, june bug, cockroach, silverfish, earwig, wasp, yellow jacket, gnat, mayfly, butterfly, moth, firefly, Africanized or killer bee, army ant, cricket

arachnids: spider, mite, daddy longlegs, black widow, trap-door spider, chigger, aphid, scorpion

crustaceans: crab, shrimp, lobster, crayfish, barnacle, wood louse

One Step Further: Ask students to sort their arthropods into categories: insects, arachnids, and crustaceans. They may need to use references to verify their answers.

_____
_____
_____
_____

38 **List as many different types of sports equipment as you can.**

Sample Solutions: baseball, bat, gloves, mitts, bases, catcher's gear, umpire's chest protector, batting helmets, basketball, hoop, net, football, helmet, goalposts, pads, official's whistle, uniforms, volleyball, volleyball net, knee pads, soccer goals, shin guards, soccer ball, tennis racquets, tennis nets, racquetball, racquetball racquets, hockey puck, hockey stick, ice skates, face masks, golf clubs, golf tees, golf carts, rollerblades, ramps, Frisbee, bobsled, skis, ski poles, skateboards, snowboard, snowmobile, snow shoes, bowling ball, bowling pins, score sheets, badminton racquet and net, badminton birdies

_____
_____
_____
_____

Suppose you have been challenged to come up with a new name for a children's cereal. The cereal is healthy so parents will love it. But the cereal maker wants children to like it, too. Come up with several names for the new cereal along with a slogan or two for each new name.

Sample Solutions:

Galaxy: You'll be a star with our new cereal. Blast off to a great day with Galaxy!

Odds and Ends: A little bit of everything you've always loved for breakfast. End your boredom and up your odds for a great day!

Great Flake Surprise: You'll be surprised at the great taste! You won't be a flake when you eat our flakes.

39

___

What materials, other than wood, could you use to make a picture frame?

Sample Solutions: cardboard, fabric, Styrofoam meat tray, duct tape, heavy rope, yarn, metal coat hanger, glass, old photos, gift wrap, foil, beads, string

40

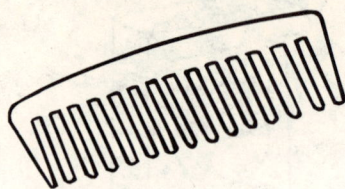

 41 **List things you would never say to a police officer.**

Sample Solutions:

"Leave me alone."

"Officer, you must be blind!"

"Shut up!"

"Get lost."

"Who do you think you are?"

"Who put you in charge?"

"Why should I listen to you?"

"Do you want to make me?"

"Let's settle this right here, right now."

"Wait until I get my hands on you!"

"Do I look like I want to talk to you?"

"I don't get mad—I get even."

"If you don't leave me alone, my dad will call your supervisor!"

_____

_____

_____

 42 **Make a list of products that would be useless for someone who is completely bald.**

Sample Solutions: Shampoo, conditioner, hairspray, hair gel, hair dryer, curling iron, hair color, comb, brush, barrettes, ribbons, ponytail holders, extensions, gift certificate to hair salon, hair-cutting scissors

_____

_____

_____

Name as many countries as you can whose names do not use the letter *e*.

Sample Solutions: Afghanistan, Austria, Australia, Angola, Brazil, Bulgaria, Canada, China, Colombia, Costa Rica, Finland, Guyana, Haiti, Honduras, Iran, Iraq, Italy, Ivory Coast, Jamaica, Japan, Jordan, Kyrgyzstan, Kuwait, Laos, Latvia, Libya, Malaysia, Mali, Malta, Moldova, Mongolia, Monaco, Morocco, Pakistan, Poland, Portugal, Romania, Russia, Samoa, Saudi Arabia, Somalia, South Africa, Spain, Tanzania, Thailand, Tunisia, Uganda, Uruguay, Yugoslavia, Zambia

43

When is it better to be last than to be first?

Sample Solutions:

When catching the school bus in the morning. (The last one picked up has the shortest bus ride.)

When you're in an elimination competition. (The last person left is the winner.)

When you're learning something new. (You can watch everyone else do it first.)

44

2 minutes

45 **List as many foods as you can that are spelled with double letters.**

Sample Solutions: pizza, butter, waffles, blueberries, strawberries, cherries, cobbler, apples, beef, walleye, gummy bears, cabbage, spaghetti, vanilla ice cream, green pepper, beets, sunflower or pumpkin seeds, sweet potatoes, eggs, broccoli, carrots, lettuce, zucchini, coffee, cinnamon rolls

46 **What things are made of glass?**

Sample Solutions: eyeglasses, drinking glasses, mirrors, windows, light bulbs, vases, test tubes, bottles, aquariums, marbles, television and computer screens, the "glass ceiling," the part of a picture frame that protects the picture, magnifying glass, paperweights, Christmas tree ornaments

What things have handles?

Sample Solutions: purse, briefcase, tools, amusement park rides, overweight people have "love handles," drawers, mugs and teacups, safes, baskets, car doors, recliners, refrigerators, stoves, dishwashers, vacuum cleaners, a person who understands a situation is said to have a "handle" on it

47

_____
_____
_____
_____

Pretend the year is 2050. You are a lot older, and you have children and grandchildren. Tell them about the good old days when you were in school. List things that you have or do now that probably won't be around when your children and grandchildren are grown up.

48

Sample Solutions: CD-ROMs; DVD players; large desktop computers; cars that run on gasoline; cars that have to be washed and waxed; telephones without video; clear, freshwater lakes; ovens that require an entire hour to bake a loaf of bread; shortages of electricity

_____
_____
_____
_____

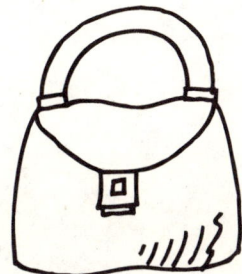

49 A fitness gym might use the acronym SWEAT in its advertising slogan, "SWEAT with us" to mean Swim, Workout, Exercise, and Train. What might the acronym HELP represent? What businesses or agencies might use it?

Sample Solutions:

Heating assistance for the Elderly, Low-Income, and Poor, used by a city assistance program

Historical Educational Learning Program, used by a public television station

Hungry? Eat here. Low Prices, used by a budget restaurant

_____
_____
_____
_____

50 List words or phrases that contain *apple*.

Sample Solutions: apple juice, apple pie, apple butter, taffy apple, apple crisp, applesauce, Adam's apple, the apple of my eye, Johnny Appleseed, apple cobbler, Apple Jacks®, apple strudel, apple cider, apple tree, apple orchard, apple dumplings, apple jelly, apple seeds, apple core, the Big Apple

_____
_____
_____
_____

Imagine that your Christmas tree can talk. What might it say to you while you are decorating it?

Sample Solutions:

"Ouch!"

"Ooooh, that looks beautiful."

"I love getting dressed up for the holidays!"

"Why do I always have to stay indoors?"

"When you cut me down, I was afraid the end was near. I'm so glad I get to live in your home now!"

"I think that ornament is really ugly."

"Hey, watch it! You almost knocked me over."

"I think my bad side is showing. Could you please turn me a little."

"I'm thirsty. Please water me."

_____
_____
_____
_____

List as many words of three or more letters as you can spell using only the letters in *hard drive*.

Sample Solutions: air, are, arid, avid, dad, dare, dear, did, dive, diver, drear, driver, ear, had, hair, hard, hare, have, head, hear, heard, herd, hid, hide, hive, rare, rave, read, rid, ride, rider, river, vie

_____
_____
_____
_____

53 **What materials from plants and animals are used to make clothing?**

Sample Solutions: Cotton fabric is made from cotton plants. Leather is made from cowhide. Linen comes from flax plants. Wool comes from sheep's fleece. Pigskin is used like leather. Some people wear skirts made of grass.

_____
_____
_____
_____

54 **The story is about a new computer virus that erases school records about students' grades and behavior. What is the headline?**

Sample Solutions: Virus Makes Principal Sick; Retrieval Begins; Irresponsibility Eroded by Erasures; School Staff Goes Back to the Drawing Board; Computer Glitch Leaves Some Students Breathing a (Hopeful) Sigh of Relief; Honor Students Concerned about Losing Scholarship Opportunities

_____
_____
_____
_____

Some things grow bigger as time goes on. A tree, for example, grows larger and larger as it ages. What things grow smaller as time passes?

Sample Solutions: a burning candle, a loaf of bread grows smaller as it is eaten, an apple grows smaller and shrivels as it ages and dries, moth balls become smaller over time, the time remaining to complete a project, bank accounts may grow smaller

55

_____
_____
_____
_____

List things that are sticky.

Sample Solutions: sticky cinnamon buns, stickers, tape, glue, lollipop, transparent tape, masking tape, superglue, maple syrup, honey, wet paint, dried fruit, chewing gum, self-adhesive stamps and labels, sweaty skin, snails, a tricky situation

56

_____
_____
_____
_____

57 **We use many idioms, such as putting your foot in your mouth, that refer to parts of the body. List as many idioms as you can that mention parts of the human body.**

Sample Solutions: kick up your heels, turn a cold shoulder, I'm all ears, get off my back, stop pulling my leg, you've got rocks in your head, we don't see eye to eye on this, you're getting on my nerves, keep a straight face, keep your head, let your hair down, play into someone's hands, turn a deaf ear

___

58 **We use many similes that include animals, such as "hungry as a horse." How many more animal similes can you list? (Remember that a simile uses *like* or *as* to compare things.)**

Sample Solutions: busy as a bee, fat as a pig, meek as a lamb, sly as a fox, strong as an ox, quiet as a mouse, stubborn as a mule, laughing like a hyena, work like a horse, drink like a fish, waddle like a duck

___

The answer is chicken soup. What is the question?

Sample Solutions: What are we having for lunch? What kind of soup is on sale at the grocery store this week? What kind of soup is recommended if you have a bad cold? What is one of America's most popular soups? What kind of soup comes after cabbage soup alphabetically? What is the brand name of a popular series of inspirational books?

_____
_____
_____
_____

Name places that begin with the letter *d*.

Sample Solutions: Denver, Dublin, Dallas, downstairs, Daytona Beach, Detroit, Dover, Des Moines, Duluth, downtown, down under, down state, down stream, down stage, drum shop, delicatessen, dump, drug store, drawbridge, desert, Delaware, Denmark, Dominican Republic

_____
_____
_____
_____

Guidelines for 5-Minute Brainstorming Activities

1. Read the teacher's notes that precede each student page.

2. Consider the suggestions in the teacher's notes to decide how to group students. Some activities are suitable for individual work; other activities work best in small groups. Suggestions for sizes of the groups is included.

3. Gather all needed materials before beginning each activity. Be sure students have blank paper and sharpened pencils, as well as the activity pages, before you begin.

4. In general, instruct each group to complete just one activity page. There may be instances, however, when you may want each person in a group to complete her or his own page. This may be useful if you think some students are not participating fully in the group.

5. Read the question clearly. Repeat it. Ask students if they understand it. If not, give a brief explanation.

6. Be clear about the starting and stopping times with your students. Also be clear about what you expect them to have accomplished at the end of the five-minute time period.

7. If at any time you feel that students are being particularly productive and creative, feel free to extend the time period beyond the five minutes.

8. Be aware that humor is an important element in brainstorming. Expect the process to often lead to funny answers—good!

9. Mention some of the sample responses given in this book if they are significantly different from your students' answers. *Please note: The sample answers provided are not intended to be a complete list of possible solutions.* Accept all reasonable answers, but always ask for clarification if an idea has not been clearly communicated. If you like, add some of your students' answers on the blank lines provided in this book. You can use them in brainstorming sessions with future groups of students.

10. During or after each brainstorming activity, you may want students to make notes in a notebook or on a log sheet. Students can record 1) the question or activity, 2) their own responses, and 3) classmates' responses they liked best. They can also leave space to write other answers that come to mind later. These notes can serve as story starters or can generate ideas for other creative writing assignments.

11. You will notice that some activities include a section called One Step Further. These are ideas for extending the activity beyond five minutes. Other activities may also come to mind as your class works through the exercises.

Teacher's Notes

Bananagrams

◆ Students consider words and their meanings from a different perspective as they brainstorm to create new words. Students may work alone or in groups of two to five students.

Materials

- One copy of the activity sheet on page 70 for each student and an extra copy for each group.
- A supply of pencils and blank paper.
- Dictionaries, one per person or one to two per group

Directions to Students

Read the directions and examples on your activity page. You will see that a *bananagram* is a brand-new word created by combining two words that share two or more letters. Be sure you understand the examples before time begins. You will have five minutes to write as many of your own bananagrams, with definitions, as you can. Use dictionaries for ideas if you wish. You may write words and definitions that are nonsensical!

- daffodiligent—a hard-working florist
- piccoloafers—comfortable shoes sold using high-pitch tactics
- stethoscopener—a device that uses sound waves to open cans
- popcornament—a homemade Christmas tree decoration
- guitarp—a protective guitar covering
- carpetals—flowery floor coverings
- dinnerves—the uneasy feelings experienced by a host prior to a party

One Step Further:

Suggest students choose one or more of their favorite bananagrams and write one-paragraph stories using them.

Name _____ Date _____

Bananagrams

bananagram: a new word that when "peeled" reveals two known words

You will brainstorm to create fun new words called *bananagrams*, along with definitions for them. A bananagram is a new word formed by two familiar words that share at least two letters. For example, the word *banana* and *anagram* were combined by overlapping the shared letters *a-n-a*. A banana is, of course, a yellow fruit with a large outer peel. An anagram is a word or phrase formed by rearranging letters of another word or phrase. You could loosely define a *bananagram*, then, as a new word that when "peeled" reveals two known words.

You could also combine the word *banana* with a different *a-n-a* or *n-a* word as shown here:

banana + *analyst* = *bananalyst*: a tropical fruit inspector

banana + *napkin* = *bananapkin*: a wrap for used banana peels

Here are two more examples:

hospital + *italics* = *hospitalics*: health care with a new slant

agent + *entertainer* = agentertainer: undercover comedian

Now it's your turn. You will have five minutes to create your own bananagrams. Use dictionaries for ideas if you wish. Write your new words and their definitions here.

_____
_____
_____
_____
_____
_____
_____
_____

Teacher's Notes

Human vs. Computer

☛ Students use their analytical skills to think about the differences in the ways humans and computers perform tasks. This activity works well with large groups of students.

Materials
- One copy of the activity sheet on page 72 for each student and an extra copy for each group
- A supply of pencils and blank paper

Directions to Students
Your group will brainstorm differences in the ways humans and computers work. A few examples will help you get started. You have five minutes to write as many comparisons as you can.

Sample Solutions:

Human	Computer
It can adapt new information to the present situation.	It works consistently with very large amounts of information.
It performs the same task in slightly different ways each time.	It performs the same task in exactly the same way every time.
It often forgets information	It can recall every piece of information it has ever received.
Partway through a task, it can change its mind and proceed another way.	It can perform many different tasks at the same time.
It can create a new outcome.	It is predictable and reliable.
It can be overwhelmed by large amounts of information.	
It may be unpredictable and unreliable.	

One Step Further
Science fiction sometimes postulates a world takeover by advanced computers. Ask students to discuss if they think such a possibility exists and why or why not.

Human vs. Computer

You will have five minutes to brainstorm differences in the ways humans and computers perform tasks. Some examples will help you get started.

Human

It performs the same task in slightly different ways each time.

It uses a lot of space to store information.

Computer

It performs the same task exactly the same way every time.

It uses a small space to store an enormous amount of information.

Teacher's Notes

Toothpick Tricks

● Students brainstorm solutions to puzzles involving toothpicks and squares. This activity is best for small groups of two or three students.

Materials

- One copy of the activity sheet on page 74 for each student and an extra copy for each group
- A supply of pencils and blank paper
- 24 toothpicks for each group or 24 narrow strips of paper. (Hold a 3"-x-5" card horizontally and slice with a paper cutter. Cut strips about 1 cm wide to yield 12–13 strips per card.)

Directions to Students

Read the instructions on the activity sheet. Arrange 24 toothpicks (or paper strips) as shown in the diagram. Then remove different toothpicks until you arrive at the correct number of squares. Sometimes there is more than one solution. Sketch the solution that you find in the space provided. For each problem, start with the arrangement shown at the top of the page.

Sample Solutions:

Name _____ Date _____

Toothpick Tricks

First arrange 24 toothpicks or paper strips in this arrangement:

Now try to solve these puzzles. You will have five minutes to remove toothpicks and form new shapes. Draw the new shapes in the spaces provided.

1. Remove 4 toothpicks and leave 5 squares.

2. Remove 6 toothpicks and leave 5 squares.

3. Remove 8 toothpicks and leave 4 squares.

Teacher's Notes

More Toothpick Tricks

→ Students arrange toothpicks to form a specific number of squares. It is suggested for this activity that students work in small groups of two or three.

Materials

- A copy of the activity sheet on page 76 for each student and an extra copy for each group.
- A supply of pencils and blank paper.
- 24 toothpicks for each group or 24 narrow strips of paper. (Hold a 3"-x-5" card horizontally and slice with a paper cutter. Cut strips about 1 cm wide to yield 12–13 strips per card.)

Directions to Students

Use 24 toothpicks (or paper strips) to form either 7 or 8 squares. You will need to use all 24 toothpicks. The squares may overlap. They do not all need to be the same size. You and your partner(s) have five minutes to complete the activity. NOTE: Be ready to add more time if you see that students are working well but have not yet found solutions. Or, you may wish to give students five minutes to solve the first problem and another five minutes to solve the second.

Sample Solutions:

1. 7 squares

2. 8 squares or

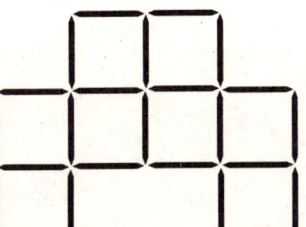 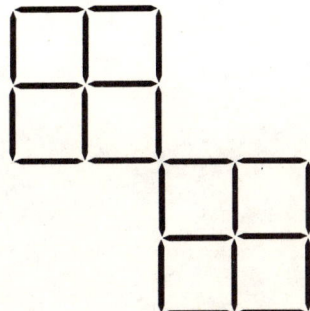

Name _____   Date _____

More Toothpick Tricks

Try your hand at more toothpick puzzlers. This time, use 24 toothpicks to form either 7 squares or 8 squares. Your final solutions use all 24 toothpicks. The squares you make may intersect and/or overlap. They do not have to be the same size. Brainstorm with your partner(s) to find possible solutions. Sketch your final answers below.

1. 24 toothpicks form exactly 7 squares

2. 24 toothpicks form exactly 8 squares

Teacher's Notes

5 minutes

Book Covers

➥ Students practice rhyming as they brainstorm new titles for well-known books. Groups of four to seven students will work well to complete this activity.

Materials

- One copy of the activity sheet on page 78 for each student and an extra copy for each group
- A supply of pencils and colored pencils and drawing paper

Directions to Students

Read the directions on the page. You will create brand-new book titles by replacing words in well-known titles with words that rhyme with the originals. Then you will select one or more titles for which to make a book cover. As a group you will complete at least one book cover design. Do just a quick, simple sketch.

Sample Solutions:

Original title	New title	Illustration ideas
War and Peace	Core and Cease	Cut-up apple with the core removed
The Two Towers	The Goo Showers	Muddy rain
Robin Hood	Blob in Wood	Strange-looking blob of putty stuck on a log
Sherlock Holmes	Pure Clock Combs	Clocks with combs for hands
Old Yeller	Cold Cellar	Someone sitting, shivering, in a basement

One Step Further

Challenge students to write a brief synopsis of one of their new stories.

5 minutes

Book Covers

You will have five minutes to work. First, quickly list titles of several books. Then brainstorm with your group to write new titles for some of them by replacing words in the original titles with words that rhyme with them. For example, if you begin with the book *Return of the King*, your new title may be *The Burn of the Ming*.

Next, collaborate with your group to design a book cover for one or more of your titles. The cover illustration should fit the new title. The book cover for *The Burn of the Ming* might include a Chinese-looking vase in a furnace. Describe or sketch your design rather than make a detailed drawing.

Write your old and new titles here.

_____   _____

_____   _____

_____   _____

Describe or draw possible book cover designs for one of your new titles.

Teacher's Notes

5 minutes

❧ Students consider nuance and other word skills as they brainstorm to write plays with different moods. Groups of three to six students work well together to share ideas.

Materials

- One copy of the activity sheet (half of page 80) for each student and an extra copy for each group
- A supply of pencils and blank paper

Happy Playwright

Directions to Students

Read the directions on your page. You will write a very brief play that uses just two characters—a cake and a candle. Your play should contain only conversation that takes place between the characters—no narration. Think of a play that is upbeat and happy.

Sample Solutions:

CAKE: Hey, Candle, will you go out with me tonight?
CANDLE: Well, that depends on where you want to go.
CAKE: I'm putting on a glam look to go to Michelle's birthday party. She's turning fourteen years old.
CANDLE: What's happening at the party?
CAKE: Everyone will play games, listen to music, give Michelle presents, and eat lots of food.
CANDLE: In that case, I'd be de-LIGHT-ed to go out with you!

Gloomy Playwright

Directions to Students

Read the directions on your page. Use the same two characters—a cake and a candle. This time, write a play that is gloomy and sad.

Sample Solutions:

CAKE: Candle, I feel too sad to go out tonight. I think I really should go, though. It's Michelle's fourteenth birthday party.
CANDLE: Why is that so sad? That sounds like it should be fun.
CAKE: Well, you see, Michelle is dying of cancer and it's the last party she'll ever have.
CANDLE: That is sad. How about if I come with you? Maybe we can do our best to make it her best party ever.

Happy Playwright

You will have five minutes to pretend that you and your partners have been commissioned to write a very short script for a play with just two characters—a cake and a candle. The script must contain all dialogue—no narration.

You are in a very good mood and decide to write a very fun, happy play. Write enough lines of the script to reveal what happens in the play. You may use this page and additional paper as needed.

_____
_____
_____
_____
_____
_____

Gloomy Playwright

You will have five minutes to pretend that you and your partners have been commissioned to write a very short script for a play with just two characters—a cake and a candle. The script must contain all dialogue—no narration.

You are in a very gloomy mood and decide to write a sad play. Write enough lines of the script to reveal what happens in the play. You may use this page and additional paper as needed.

_____
_____
_____
_____
_____
_____

Teacher's Notes

Parallelograms

➥ Students use their understanding of geometry to brainstorm parallelograms. Groups of two to four students work well for this exercise.

Materials

- One copy of the activity sheet on page 82 for each student and an extra copy for each group
- A supply of pencils and blank paper
- Geoboards and rubber bands, if available, can also be used. Solutions can then be transferred to the activity page.

Directions to Students

Carefully read the directions on your page. Be sure you know the definition of a parallelogram. As you can see, the square in the example is one parallelogram. Are other rectangles also parallelograms? As you work together, think of how other parallelograms may look.

You will have five minutes to work. During that time, you need to make one answer sheet for the group on which you draw all of your parallelograms. Notice that some shapes that look different may actually be the same shape when one is turned or flipped. Try to write only answers that are different from each other.

Sample solutions:

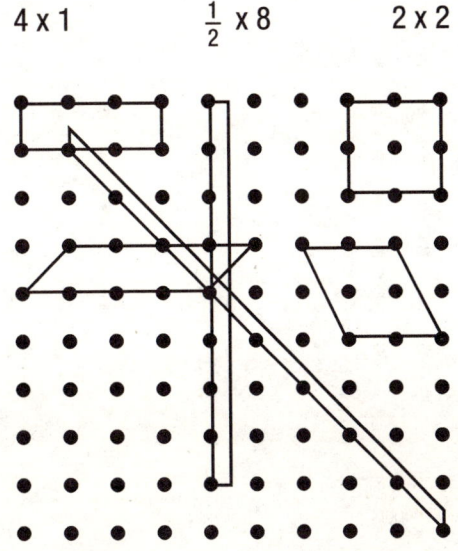

4 x 1 $\frac{1}{2}$ x 8   2 x 2

Name _____ Date _____

Parallelograms

You may already know that a parallelogram is a four-sided shape with two sets of parallel lines. You may also know that to find the area of a parallelogram, you must multiply the base by the height. Here is a parallelogram with an area of 4 square units:

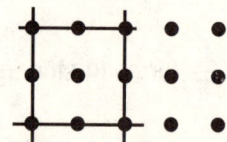

The base is 2 units. The height is 2 units. 2 x 2 = 4 square units.

Use this dot paper to draw more parallelograms with an area of 4 square units. You may also work on a geoboard first. Hint: The angles in a parallelogram do not have to be right angles.

Teacher's Notes

5 minutes

9

Inventive Match-Up

◆ Students think about objects in creative ways as they brainstorm to produce brand-new inventions. Groups of three to six students work well for this activity.

Materials

✎ One copy of the activity sheet on page 84 for each student and an extra copy for each group

✎ A supply of pencils and drawing paper

Directions to Students

Read the directions on your activity page. You will use an idea from column 1 and incorporate it with an item listed in column 2. You do not have to describe your new product in technical details, nor do you have to use the first item exactly as it exists now. Use just the features you need.

You will have five minutes to work. You may want to jot down your own ideas and then pool your ideas into a final list with your group. You may also decide to illustrate one or more of your ideas. It is up to your group to decide how to use the time.

Sample Answers

1. Equip a stapler with a small vacuum device that would automatically vacuum up any spare staples or bits of paper around it.

2. Mount cordless phones and staplers on a skateboard. Then the phone and other office equipment could be rolled easily among people who are sharing a large office.

3. Bar codes could be automatically linked to a calendar. At the first of every month, for example, prices could be set to go up 1% without a person doing it manually.

4. Cordless phones could all be equipped with Velcro so that people who move around a lot could keep the phones stuck to their clothing.

One Step Further

Keep students' ideas on file. More drawings or models could be made for art or science projects.

Name _____ Date _____

Inventive Match-Up

You will have five minutes to invent a brand-new product. Choose something from column 1 and apply some idea from it to an item in column 2. Add one or two of your own products to each column if you wish. Write your new inventions at the bottom of the page.

Example: Use the principles from a stethoscope in a sensor on a lawn mower. When the sensor detects sounds (from people, animals, other equipment) it changes the path of the lawn mower to avoid the source of the sound.

1	2
calendar	lawn mower
clothes iron	sewing machine
skateboard	airplane
stethoscope	stapler
vacuum cleaner	telephone
skyscraper	bar-code system
paper clip	computer
Velcro	space shuttle
_____	_____
_____	_____

New Ideas:

_____

_____

_____

_____

If you have time, sketch or describe one of your new ideas on another piece of paper.

Teacher's Notes

Funny Phone Numbers

➤ Students look at words and letters from a different perspective as they brainstorm words or phrases by using the letters on the telephone keypad, which is illustrated on the student page. Small groups of two to four students work well for this exercise.

Materials
- One copy of the activity sheet on page 86 for each student and an extra copy for each group
- A supply of pencils

Directions to Students
Read the instructions at the top of the page. Notice the telephone keypad. Work carefully through the example to be sure you understand how the words are used to spell phone numbers. Then brainstorm to come up with possible words or phrases for each type of business listed. Write the letters of your word or phrase, hyphenated as a phone number. You may write more than one answer for each business. Notice that the keypad has no numbers for the letters Q or Z.

Sample Answers:
1. car dealer 1-800-NEW-CARS
2. fast-food restaurant EAT-FAST
3. sports arena 1-BAS-KET-BALL; 1-PLA-YHO-CKEY
4. dentist's office 1-800-BIG-GRIN
5. hair salon CUT-HAIR; GOO-DCUT
6. dollar store ONE-BUCK, BAR-GAIN
7. computer store WIN-DOWS; 1-800-FIX-MYPC
8. teen's clothing shop GET-COOL; NUJ-EANS
9. grocery store SAV-MUCH; BUY-FOOD
10. convenience store ONE-STOP; GAS-FOOD

Name _____ Date _____

Funny Phone Numbers

```
 1      2 ABC   3 DEF
 4 GHI  5 JKL   6 MNO
 7 PRS  8 TUV   9 WXY
 *      0       #
```

You have noticed that companies sometimes use their phone numbers to spell words related to their products. You will have five minutes to think of phone numbers that reflect the nature of particular businesses. For example, a florist might advertise its phone number as FLOWERS. By checking the diagram of the telephone keypad, you can see that the phone number is 356-9377.

Now think of a word or phrase that each business below might turn into a phone number. Notice that the keypad has no numbers for the letters Q or Z. Make your words fit one of these patterns:

XXX-XXXX, 1-800-XXX-XXXX, 1-XXX-XXX-XXXX

1. car dealer _____
2. fast-food restaurant _____
3. sports arena _____
4. dentist's office _____
5. hair salon _____
6. dollar store _____
7. computer store _____
8. teen's clothing shop _____
9. grocery store _____
10. convenience store _____

If time allows, convert your words/phrases into phone numbers. Exchange papers with another brainstorming group and decode each other's words.

Teacher's Notes

◆► Students brainstorm to create a list of possible solutions to specific problems. Groups of three to seven students can work together.

Materials

✎ One copy of the activity sheet (half of page 88) for each student and an extra copy for each group

✎ A supply of pencils and blank paper

Directions to Students

Read the instructions on your page. Note the specific problem you are to solve. You will have five minutes to brainstorm. Your group may decide to brainstorm individually for the first one to two minutes and then pool ideas, or you may decide to work together for the entire five-minute period. It is your choice. Your group should come up with one list of answers. It's okay to list solutions that are unusual, ridiculous, or even impossible.

How Can We . . . ?

Imagine that you and your brainstorming group are a student advisory committee at your school. By mistake, the school receives five thousand kazoos that it did not order. The company that sent them does not want them returned. How can you put the noisemakers to good use in your school? You and your committee brainstorm possible uses for the kazoos.

Sample solutions:

Start a kazoo choir and put on kazoo concerts in nearby nursing homes and preschools. Sell the kazoos as a school fundraiser. Contact other schools and try to exchange the kazoos for art supplies or other needed items. Use the kazoos as incentives for good grades—give one to each student the first time he or she scores 100% on a quiz, until supplies run out.

How Can We . . . ?

Your neighbor is hospitalized, and you must give the neighbor's horse fresh food and water every morning. You are, however, extremely allergic to horses. You cannot touch the horse or even go in the stable. How can you care for this animal? Brainstorm ways to get food and water to the horse.

Sample solutions:

Put feed on the back of a dump truck; dump a little out every morning, throwing it over the fence. Water the horse with a hose, using a lot of water pressure that will make it spray from a distance into the trough. Borrow haz-mat gear from your local fire department. Of course, you'll terrify the horse.

Name _____ Date _____

11 How Can We . . . ?

Imagine that you and your brainstorming group are a student advisory committee at your school. By mistake, the school receives five thousand kazoos that it did not order. The company that sent them does not want them returned. How can you put the noisemakers to good use in your school? You and your committee brainstorm possible uses for the kazoos.

_____
_____
_____
_____
_____
_____
_____
_____

12 How Can We . . . ?

Your neighbor is hospitalized, and you must give the neighbor's horse fresh food and water every morning. You are, however, extremely allergic to horses. You cannot touch the horse or even go in the stable. How can you care for this animal? Brainstorm ways to get food and water to the horse.

_____
_____
_____
_____
_____
_____
_____
_____

Teacher's Notes

Astronaut

▶ Students use their analytical skills to brainstorm what makes a person suited for an unusual profession. Students can work alone or in groups of two to four. After two minutes, tell students to stop working on the first question and go to the second question.

Materials

- One copy of the activity sheet on page 90 for each student and an extra copy for each group
- A supply of pencils and blank paper

Directions to Students

Read the information on your activity sheet. You will have two minutes to brainstorm and answer the first question and three minutes for the second question.

Sample Solutions:

1. courage, intelligence, education, curiosity, math and science skills, intuition, training, ability to work on a team, perfect health, able to manage stress, calm, detail oriented

2. If control-panel alarms sound, what are the first three things you would do?

    Give an example of a situation that caused you stress and tell what you did to alleviate it.

    Challenge: a training course with obstacles and unpredictable events

    Do you consider yourself a "big-picture" person or a detail person?

    What role do you usually take on a team?

    What do you think is the bravest thing you've ever done?

Name _____ Date _____

Astronaut

You will have two minutes to brainstorm with your group and choose what you consider are the top characteristics and qualifications of the perfect astronaut. Consider what makes a person well-suited for this unusual profession. Is it knowledge, training, personality traits, or a combination of these?

_____   _____
_____   _____
_____   _____
_____   _____

If you were considering prospective astronaut candidates, what are some questions or challenges you can create to discover if they have the characteristics you listed above? You will have three minutes to come up with as many questions/challenges as you can.

_____
_____
_____
_____
_____

Teacher's Notes

Taking Off

◆◆ Students brainstorm fictional experiences in space. This activity includes small-group and individual work.

Materials

✎ One copy of the activity sheet on page 92 for each student and an extra copy for each group

✎ A supply of pencils and blank paper

Directions to Students

You will have five minutes to brainstorm what your group members know about living conditions in space for the early astronauts and then write a few sentences of a first-person account about one or two of the activities listed in part 2.

Sample Solutions:

1. tight quarters, weightlessness (affects eating, drinking, elimination, muscle strength, etc.), have to provide own oxygen, can't get away from your crewmates, can't stretch out to sleep, need to keep warm means wearing environmental suit most or all of the time

2. (leaving the launchpad) I couldn't help but hold my breath as we felt the power of the engines begin to lift the rocket skyward with us two puny people perched at the nose. All my training and preparation kept me from feeling the terror anyone in my position should feel. It seemed forever before I heard the squawk of Mission Control on the radio—forever before I took a breath, forever before I felt or heard anything but the force of the engines.

   (eating your first meal in space) "This is getting old fast," I said as I sucked my pureed mystery meat through the feeding tube. "It's supposed to be steak, but it's lacking something."

   "Just think," said Mona, "we actually looked forward to this! We thought it would be a great adventure."

   "Well," I smiled, "it is kind of fun. You know, like camping out is fun. Bad food, bad sleep—but fun."

One Step Further

Suggest students use their sentences as story starters for short stories of three or four paragraphs.

Name _____ Date _____

Taking Off

You will have five minutes to brainstorm what you know about living conditions in space for the early astronauts and to write a few sentences about one or two of the activities listed in part 2.

1. Living conditions in space:

    Examples: tight quarters, weightlessness

    _____
    _____
    _____
    _____
    _____
    _____

2. Imagine that you are one of the very first astronauts, encountering many unusual and difficult circumstances. Choose at least one activity from the following list and write a few sentences as if you were telling about your experience.

leaving the launchpad

eating your first meal in space

moving about in the space capsule

catching your first close-up glimpse of the moon

exploring the moon in a rover

performing scientific experiments

walking outside the spacecraft

seeing earth from space

changing clothes

writing a letter

docking with a foreign spacecraft

landing back on earth

deciding whether or not to make another flight

_____
_____
_____

Teacher's Notes

5 minutes

Whatchamacallit?

➥ Students brainstorm about a strange-looking object. They will decide what its purpose could be. This activity is suitable for individuals or groups of two to four students.

Materials

- One copy of the activity sheet on page 94 for each student and an extra copy for each group
- A supply of pencils and blank paper
- Rulers and stencils, if desired

Directions to Students

Look at the object on your page. Your job is to imagine what it could be. Brainstorm about its purpose, name, and so on. You may use your pencil (and rulers and stencils, if available) to add more features to this object. Then answer the questions at the bottom of the page. You will have five minutes to complete this activity.

Sample Solutions:

Please note that students' responses do not need to be technically accurate or even possible!

1. What purpose does this object serve? It is a high-tech insulated coffee mug.

2. What is it called? Antigravity Beverage Maker

3. How does it work? Water is suctioned up through the bottom trapezoid into the insulated chamber. Instant coffee is injected through the lower left rectangle. A small turbine hidden inside mixes the two. The two triangles in front form the handle. The spout on the left allows you to pour out some of the coffee to share with a friend.

4. How much does it cost? $59.95

5. Where is it sold? In fine department stores everywhere

Name _____ Date _____

Whatchamacallit?

Here is an unusual-looking object. As you look at it, brainstorm about what its purpose might be. Then answer the questions below.

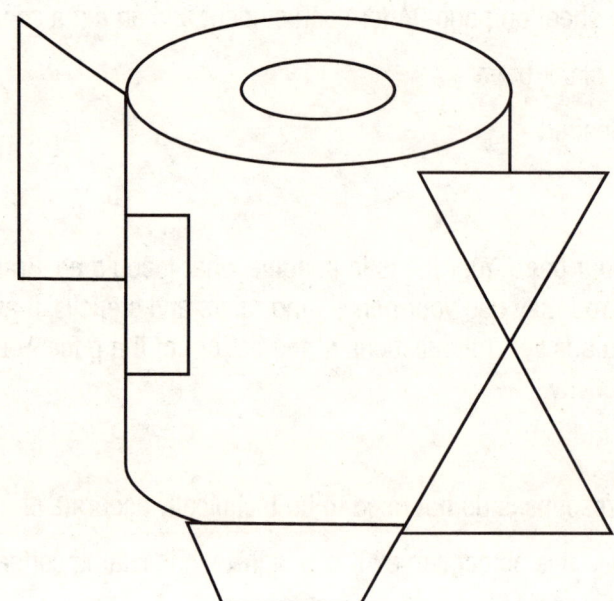

1. What purpose does this object serve?

2. What is it called?

3. How does it work?

4. How much does it cost?

5. Where is it sold?

Teacher's Notes

Hometown Café Lunch

☛ Students work on fraction and decimal relationships. Groups of two to four work well for this activity.

Materials

- One copy of the activity sheet on page 96 for each student and an extra copy for each group
- A supply of pencils and blank paper
- Geoboards and rubber bands for each student
- Calculators—one or more for each group

Directions to Students

Read the directions on the activity page. For each part of the activity, use the geoboards first. (Hint: Think of each square as a dime.) Then check your answers with a calculator.

Sample Solutions:

1. Kyla: chef's salad, milk, ice cream; Carmen: pasta plate, soft drink, pie (other answers are possible)
2. Nick could have had chef's salad, milk, and ice cream for $3.75.
3. Answers will vary.

One Step Further

Use the geoboards. How much would you get for five days if you earn $1 on the first day and double the previous day's amount every day after? What would you earn on the sixth day? What would be your total earnings after seven days? (Hint: Start with one small square as $1.00.)

Name _____ Date _____

Hometown Café Lunch

Use the geoboards first for each part of the activity. (Hint: Think of each square as a dime.) Then check your answers with a calculator.

Hometown Café Menu
- Chef's Salad ... $2.25
- Pasta Plate $4.50
- Chicken Sandwich $3.25
- Fish Taco $2.50
- Milk .... $ .65
- Pie $1.50
- Soft Drink .... $ .75
- Ice Cream .... $ .85

1. Kyla and Carmen went to the Hometown Café for lunch. Kyla's complete meal cost more than $\frac{1}{2}$ of Carmen's. What did each order? (On your group answer sheet, show what each ate and the total cost for each meal.)

Kyla   **Carmen**

_____   _____
_____   _____
_____   _____
_____   _____
_____   _____

2. Nick and Angelo had lunch at the café, too. They spent nearly $10.00 total for their two meals. Nick's meal cost about $\frac{1}{3}$ of the total. What could Nick have had for lunch?

3. Brainstorm with your group to make up some sample meals. What fractional part of $10.00 does each one cost? Example: fish taco and soft drink: 0.30 of the geoboards shows $3.00.

_____
_____
_____
_____

Teacher's Notes

Weather Wizard

➡ Students delineate company responsibilities, brainstorm a great discovery, plan ways to convince people it works, develop a marketing plan, and design advertising for it. Groups must be at least four people.

Materials

- One copy of activity 17 on page 98 for each student and an extra copy for each group
- A supply of pencils and blank paper
- Stapler(s)

Directions to Students

Read the directions on the activity page. Before timing starts, quickly decide who will fill each position in your company. Then you will have five minutes for each department to complete its assignment. When you have completed your individual work, compile all your information and staple it together in one "business plan."

Sample Solutions:

R&D: Discovered by accident, works by using a satellite; discovered by scientists working with computer models and new weather measurement devices, works by measuring many weather criteria and comparing them to historical data; discovered it while talking about thermodynamics over pizza one night, works by conduction coil modulation

Public Relations: Special events to demonstrate Weather Wizard at open-air sporting events and celebrity weddings

Marketing: Trademark the name and patent the technology or process and market it on TV and news as "the only weather that's all right all the time"; market it to national news stations; market it to brides through wedding planners and brides' magazines

Advertising:

Weather Wizard

Imagine your group is a company that has found a way to predict weather with complete accuracy. Quickly decide who will head research and development, who will be in charge of public relations, who will be marketing manager, and who will be advertising director. (If your group is more than four people, some departments can have cochairs share the duties.) Departments will have to collaborate to accomplish the tasks below in five minutes.

Research and Development: On a separate paper, tell how you made the discovery and how it works.

Public Relations: On a separate paper, tell how you plan to convince skeptics that the invention works.

Marketing: This discovery/invention can make you all rich. On a separate paper, tell how you plan to market your idea and protect it from competitors.

Advertising: On a separate paper, sketch an ad campaign for your discovery, including ads for print, television, radio, or whatever other media you wish to use.

Teacher's Notes

5 minutes

18

More Weather Wizardry

Students consider the pros and cons of using a technical marvel.

Materials

- One copy of activity 18 on page 100 for each student and an extra copy for each group
- A supply of pencils and blank paper

Directions to Students

Read the directions on the activity page. Then answer the questions. Be sure to watch the time so that you can brainstorm all three questions.

Sample Solutions:

1. **advantages** eliminate floods and droughts, eliminate famine by having good crop weather, eliminate uncertainty, cut clothing expense, travel agencies could assure travelers of good weather

2. **disadvantages:** a lot of work keeping everything in balance; even bad weather has some good outcomes for some people; couldn't keep everyone happy—farmers need rain, golfers don't want it; no variety; who decides who actually gets to control it?

3. **yes** good weather for our events, give good weather to everyone, eliminate deaths that result from bad weather

   no unforeseen results of tampering with nature and altering natural cycles and animal species, people would be mad or competing for weather they wanted, too much power for anyone, would miss the changing of the seasons, would get less enjoyment from the good weather because there would be no bad weather to make us appreciate the good

Name _____ Date _____

More Weather Wizardry

Suppose that you not only can predict the weather but can control it. You have five minutes to brainstorm the answers to the following questions.

1. List as many advantages as you can of being able to control the weather.

   _____
   _____
   _____

2. List as many disadvantages as you can of being able to control the weather.

   _____
   _____
   _____

3. If only your group or "company" had the ability to control the weather, would you want to? Why or why not?

   _____
   _____
   _____

Teacher's Notes

Recipes

☛ Students brainstorm ingredients needed for various nonfood items. They can work together in groups of two to five.

Materials

- One copy of the activity sheet on page 102 for each student and an extra copy for each group
- A supply of pencils and blank paper
- A few recipes cut out of the newspaper, or a small cookbook, for each group

Directions to Students

Read the instructions on your activity sheet. You will brainstorm to create brand-new recipes for nonfood items. Read through all three steps before time starts to be sure you understand the procedures you are to follow. At the end of five minutes, your group should have one completed recipe on the activity sheet.

Sample Solutions:

Recipe for Success

- 3 cups of determination
- 1 cup of support from others
- 2 cups of perseverance
- 2 cups of education

Stir all ingredients together. Bake in an oven warmed by a sense of humor for 5 to 50 years.

Recipe for a Terrible TV Commercial

- 2 singing rolls of toilet paper
- 1 clown in a purple wig
- 32 measures of corny music

Throw all ingredients together. Then push the mixture way to the back of the fridge and hope no one finds it!

One Step Further

Ask students to recopy their recipes on large lined recipe cards. Compile in a loose-leaf classroom "cookbook." (More recipes may be added later.) Or, post the recipes on a Web site or on a bulletin board headed, *Look What We're Cooking!*

Name _____ Date _____

Recipes

This is your chance to cook up some original recipes. But you won't be creating food! You will have just five minutes to work, so work quickly with your partners through the following steps.

1. Look at the topics listed below, then choose one of them. (Or you may pick another similar title of your own.) Think about what ingredients might be necessary to create your recipe.
    - Recipe for Success
    - Recipe for Friendship
    - Recipe for Disaster
    - Recipe for a Happy Family
    - Recipe for Good Grades
    - Recipe for Safety
    - Recipe for a Great TV Show
    - Recipe for a Terrible TV Commercial

2. Next, quickly glance at some real recipes to see how they are written. Notice words like *stir*, *blend*, *bake*, *chop*, and other cooking terms.

3. Finally, write your complete recipe here, including the title.

_____
_____
_____
_____
_____
_____
_____

Teacher's Notes

Give Me Five!

◆◆ Students look at numbers from a different perspective as they brainstorm to create equations. This is a good independent activity, or you may choose to use it with pairs of students.

Materials

- One copy of the activity sheet on page 104 for each student and one extra copy for each pair or group
- A supply of pencils and blank paper
- (Optional) Calculators, one or more for each pair or group

Directions to Students

On this activity page you will write math sentences that result in the answers shown. Notice the guidelines for your equations.

- You may use up to five 5s.
- The 5s can be written next to each other or separated by +, -, x, ÷, or ( ).

Be sure you understand these, as well as the example equation, before time begins.

Sample Solutions:

1. $(5 \div 5) + 5 = 6$
2. $(55 \div 5) + 5 = 16$
3. $55 - 5 = 50$
4. $(5 \times 5) + (55 - 5) = 75$
5. $555 \div 5 = 111$
6. $(5 \times 5 \times 5) + 5 = 130$
7. $555 - (5 \times 5) = 530$
8. $555 + 55 = 610$
9. $55 \times (55 - 5) = 2750$

Name _____ Date _____

Give Me Five!

Your challenge is to find as many of the answers below as possible by using only the number 5 in your equations. For example, this equation uses only 5s to equal 30:

(5 x 5) + 5 = 30

- You may use up to five 5s.
- The 5s can be written next to each other or separated by +, -, x, ÷, or ( ).

You will have five minutes to solve as many as you can.

1. _____ = 6
2. _____ = 16
3. _____ = 50
4. _____ = 75
5. _____ = 111
6. _____ = 130
7. _____ = 530
8. _____ = 610
9. _____ = 2750

Teacher's Notes

You're Late!

◆◆ Students think creatively as they brainstorm excuses for being late. Students can work alone or in groups of two to six.

Materials

✎ One copy of the activity sheet on page 106 for each student and an extra copy for each group

✎ A supply of pencils and blank paper

Directions to Students

Read the directions on your activity page. Notice that you are to invent excuses—either reasonable or ridiculous—for being late in many different situations. You will have five minutes to list your best reason on each line. (Groups should compile one answer page for the entire group.)

Sample Solutions:

1. I'm sorry, sir, that I could not see you last week and remove this tooth before the infection spread throughout your body. You see, I was working on Mrs. Downs's dentures. As I was repairing them and gluing a new tooth on her upper plate, I accidentally picked up the wrong adhesive. The glue leaked out of the tube onto my index finger. The new denture tooth had to be surgically removed from my finger; then my finger had to be stitched. Just today I had the stitches removed, and my doctor gave me permission to come back to work.

7. I would have been here before you closed, but the sunroof flew open on my car when I was just three blocks from home. I turned around (since it was raining) and asked my neighbor (who happens to be handy at that sort of thing) to fix it. Then I hit four red traffic lights in a row. As I was sailing through the fifth (which, finally, was green) I heard a thumping noise from my left rear tire. Sure enough, it was flat. I pushed my car one more block to the nearest gas station where someone (very kindly and as quickly as possible) changed my tire. Then, just as I was leaving the station, I ran out of gas. So, again I pushed my car back to the station, looked around the floor for spare change (because I'd just given the person who fixed the flat the last cash I had) and found six quarters, to buy enough gas to get here. And then I drove here and you were closed. Please let me mail my envelope!

Name _____ Date _____

You're Late!

In this exercise, you will have five minutes to write an excuse that someone in a certain situation might give for being late. Choose one of the people listed below. Write a five- or six-sentence explanation (excuse) the tardy person might give to the other person(s) mentioned. Your reasons may be rather reasonable or totally ridiculous. If you have extra time, try writing an excuse for a second person on the list. Use another piece of paper if you need it.

1. You are a dentist who is too late in removing a bad tooth and your patient becomes ill.

2. You are a hairdresser who is too late in washing out hair color and your client's hair turns purple.

3. You are an Olympic athlete who is too late for the start of a race for which you have trained for three years.

4. You are a baker who is late in taking a wedding cake out of the oven, and it's burned. There's not enough time to make a new one before the wedding.

5. You are late for a party you are hosting. Your guests wonder if they should go home.

6. You are a newspaper writer who finishes a story too late to get it into the day's paper. Your boss is not happy.

7. You arrive at the post office too late to mail your annual tax return. You plead with the postal worker to unlock the door and accept the envelope.

Teacher's Notes

Mystery Writer

◆◆ Students brainstorm to concoct a mystery story using a few clues. Groups of three to seven students should work on this activity.

Materials

- One copy of the activity sheet on page 108 for each student and an extra copy for each group
- A supply of pencils and blank paper

Directions to Students

On the activity page, you will find the clues to a mystery. Think about how these clues can all fit together in a story. Write a synopsis of your story idea. Each group will complete one sheet together.

Sample Solution: A gang has been breaking into homes and businesses, stealing computers, monitors, printers, and other accessories. They become bolder with every break-in. They bragged to a newspaper in an anonymous letter that they always leave a clue to their next strike. Police have found a house where the crooks have been hiding. No one is home, but a shamrock and a book with a missing page are found. A detective notices that the book is a business directory and the missing page lists area pubs and clubs. The shamrock tips him off to expect the next hold up to be at the Irish Pub on Main Street.

One Step Further

Have students expand their synopses to complete stories with characters, dialogue, etc.

Name _____   Date _____

Mystery Writer

Read these clues about a mystery story. Brainstorm with others in your group to decide what the mystery is about. Write a synopsis of your mystery.

> The detective knew the mystery could be solved using the clues discovered in a book. First, pages 203–4 had been torn out of the book. Secondly, there was a shamrock pressed between the front cover and first page of the book. Tell what the mystery was about, what the clues meant, and how the case was solved.

_____
_____
_____
_____
_____
_____
_____
_____
_____
_____
_____
_____
_____
_____
_____

Teacher's Notes

How Do You Get Rid of Water?

➡ Students brainstorm ways to get rid of excess objects. They can work in groups of three to six people.

Material

- One copy of the activity sheet (half of page 110) for each student and an extra copy for each group
- A supply of pencils and blank paper

Directions to Students

Read the problem on your activity sheet. You will have five minutes to brainstorm ways to get rid of water and list as many as you can. Choose one person to write answers for the group. Use extra paper if you need it.

Sample Solutions: Place a hose in the tub and run it out the window, then suck on the other end of the hose with a vacuum (or your mouth) to get the water flowing out. Assuming the water is clean, invite neighborhood children over and give them drinking straws; they could drink as much water as they liked until the tub was empty. Use a turkey baster to siphon the water into pots and pans.

How Do You Get Rid of Peas?

Directions to Students

Read the problem on your activity sheet. You will have five minutes to brainstorm ways to get rid of peas and list as many as you can. Choose one person to write answers for the group. Use extra paper if you need it.

Sample Solutions: Create new recipes using a lot of peas (such as pea-pod pie or pea-pod stew) and then sell your products from a stand on your front lawn. Divide the peas into plastic grocery bags and give them to a charity food bank to distribute.

How Do You Get Rid of Water?

You have five minutes to brainstorm ways that you can empty a bathtub full of water. The drain is plugged and you have no buckets to bail out the water. List as many ideas as you can.

_____
_____
_____
_____
_____
_____
_____
_____

How Do You Get Rid of Peas?

You have five minutes to brainstorm ways to get rid of five hundred bushels of pea pods. You cannot sell the peas wholesale to a large processing company. Find ways to use them in smaller amounts. List as many ideas as you can.

_____
_____
_____
_____
_____
_____
_____
_____

Teacher's Notes

Punny Books

◆◆ Students brainstorm to create book titles and authors that contain puns and other humorous words. Students should work in small groups of two or three.

Materials

✎ One copy of the activity sheet on page 112.
✎ A supply of pencils and blank paper.

Directions to Students

Read the directions and examples on your activity sheet. You will invent some puns for titles and authors of books. First brainstorm with your partner(s) to think of authors' names that could become part of a pun or descriptive word. After creating an author's name, you can create a title that works well with it.

Sample Solutions:

Dick Shunarry, *The English Language*; Bea Flatt, *Learn to Read Music*; Terry Cloth, *Beach Towels Galore*; Phil A. Delphia, *Pennsylvania Cities*; Justin Time, *Learn to Be Punctual*; Penny Buck, *Bank Teller's Manual*

Name _____   Date _____

Punny Books

Your challenge in this activity is to create titles and authors for some "punny" books. Here are some examples:

Foo Young, *Oriental Egg Recipes*

R. U. Here, *Studies on School Attendance*

Tim Ber, *The History of Lumberjacking*

How many more titles and authors can you list for some "punny" books? You may want to brainstorm authors' names and then decide what titles you can make up to go with them. You will have five minutes in which to work. Write your author names and new book titles here.

_____
_____
_____
_____
_____
_____
_____

Teacher's Notes

5 minutes

Mystery Box

➥ Students brainstorm to determine what might be in the mystery boxes. They may work alone or in groups of two to six people.

Materials

- One copy of the activity sheet (half of page 114) for each student and an extra copy for each group
- A supply of pencils and blank paper

Directions to Students

You will have five minutes to brainstorm and write ideas about what might be in the mystery box. Read the description carefully. Then list as many different ideas as you can. If you are working in a group, list best ideas on one sheet for the entire group. Use extra paper if you need it.

Sample Solutions: 1) large magnets—your science teacher picked them up from a supply store where they were wrapped, set them on your desk, but was interrupted before putting them put away; 2) some small weights meant for the athletic department's weight machines; 3) gold bars that were smuggled in a box of textbooks.

Mystery Box II

Directions to Students

You will have five minutes to brainstorm and write ideas about what might be in the mystery box. Read the description carefully. Then list as many different ideas as you can. If you are working in a group, list best ideas on one sheet for the entire group. Use extra paper if you need it.

Sample Solutions: 1) TBA means Total Blast Attitude; the company is sending you free copies of their new CD release for you and your friends to review, along with a display to put up in school. 2) TBA means Toledo Bowling Association; it is sending you new bowling uniforms for your leagues' teams. The president of your league ordered them and forgot to tell you they were coming to your house. 3) TBA means Today's Best Advertisements. The company has chosen your name at random to receive a huge assortment of sample products from many different manufacturers.

Name _____ Date _____

Mystery Box

Imagine that a mysterious box is sitting on top of your desk. It is about the size of a shoe box. It is wrapped in plain brown paper. There is no writing on the paper. You try to lift the box, but it is too heavy. What could be in the box? Write your ideas in this space and on additional paper as needed.

Mystery Box II

Imagine that a large box is delivered to you at home. It is in the shape of a cube. Each side is about 5 feet long. The box is addressed to you. This is the return address on the box:

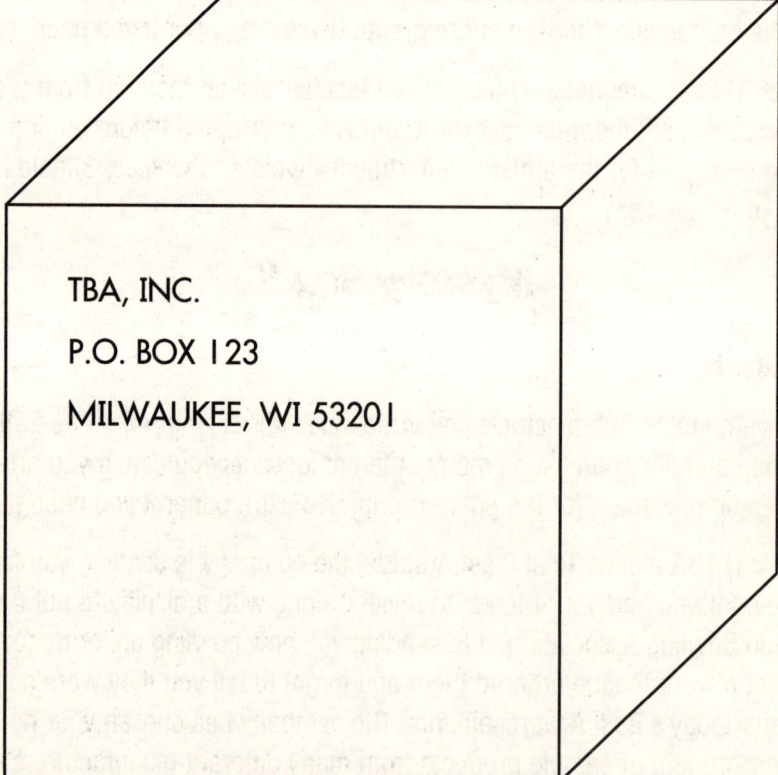

TBA, INC.
P.O. BOX 123
MILWAUKEE, WI 53201

What could be in the box? What is the TBA company? Write your ideas in this space and on additional paper as needed.

Teacher's Notes

Props and Plots

🔑 Students think creatively about objects as they brainstorm scripts. Groups of three to six work well for this exercise.

Materials

- One copy of the activity sheet on page 116 for each student and an extra copy for each group
- A supply of pencils and blank paper

Directions to Students

You will have five minutes to read the lists of props and then decide on movie plots that require all of the objects in each group. Describe your plots in one to three sentences each, as in the example. You may create more than one plot per set of props if you like. (Use the back of your sheet for additional space, if necessary.) Your group should complete one page together. Try to write plots for at least six lists of props.

Sample Solutions:

1. The movie is a western in which a doctor diagnoses a young child with a terminal disease. Thankfully, the child lives beyond the Christmas holidays.

2. A middle-aged piano teacher searches for new dreams of her own as her only child leaves home to become an astronaut and her husband spends more and more time at the office.

3. This comedy features a curious infant who climbs out of its stroller while on a trip to the zoo. The infant pulls the tail of a live skunk and crawls onto the back of an alligator.

4. This mystery begins at an amusement park where the safe is broken into. A large amount of cash is stolen. A few bills are found strewn about the water slide. The cash is later recovered in a furniture store, inside the works of a large grandfather clock.

5. In this tragic tale about Alzheimer's disease, the main character breaks a mirror but doesn't remember doing so and repeatedly blames others in the household. He is always losing his eyeglasses. Finally, he acknowledges that he is losing his memory. He becomes fond of looking up even the simplest facts in an encyclopedia to be sure he's thinking correctly.

Name _____ Date _____

Props and Plots

Lights, camera, action! Listed below are ten sets of props. Suppose that each set of items is required for a different movie. You will have five minutes to brainstorm a plot that fits each set of props. You may write more than one answer for each set of props. Try to write responses for at least six of the lists in the time allowed.

Example: globe, camera, pair of dirty socks—In this documentary, a photographer travels to every continent filming native people and customs. Often he walks for days at a time with no stops for bathing or laundry.

1. western boots, stethoscope, candy cane _____

2. spaceship, piano, briefcase _____

3. alligator, skunk, baby stroller _____

4. grandfather clock, waterslide, large bag of cash _____

5. broken mirror, encyclopedia, eyeglasses _____

6. tractor, speed boat, laundry basket _____

7. jar of marbles, satellite dish, cat _____

8. hair dryer, American flag, radio _____

9. weight set, swimming pool, uniform _____

10. sink, typewriter, poodle _____

Teacher's Notes

Greeting Cards

➥ Students brainstorm to create appropriate greeting card verses for some unusual events. For this activity, they may work in groups of two to four.

Materials:

- One copy of the activity sheet on page 118 for each student and an extra copy for each group
- A supply of pencils, pens, markers, and crayons, and colored paper

Directions to Students

You have five minutes to create a unique greeting card. Read through the lists on your sheet of occasions, senders, and recipients. Then choose one from each category and write an appropriate greeting card verse. Your verses do not have to rhyme. Design an illustration for the outside of the greeting card. Write the words on the inside. Each group should work together to complete one card.

Sample Solutions:

1. Happy Birthday to Mr. Potato Head from Mrs. Potato Head:

    Whether I'm peeled, baked, mashed, or fried
    My love for you has never died.
    Happy Birthday, Spud!

2. Happy First of August to the teachers from the principal:

    May your First of August be hot and bright,
    A memory to last through that first parent-teacher night.

3. Happy Stinky Feet Day to Mom from your son:

    Congrats, you with stinky feet.
    I sure think they're pretty neat;
    You got them 'cause you work so hard
    Paying off my credit card.

Name _____ Date _____

Greeting Cards

Imagine that your group has just been hired by the most innovative greeting card company in America. You have been asked to create an unusual card. Select one occasion along with one sender and one recipient from the lists below. Write verse ideas and sketch illustrations on the bottom and back of this page. You will have five minutes to complete your design.

Occasions

Birthday	Great-Aunt's Day	Justin Timberlake's Birthday
Snow Day	The First of August	Hat Day
New Pillows Day	Stinky Feet Day	(you invent one) _____

Recipients and Senders

To Mom/Dad from your son/daughter	To Aunt Frieda from little Billy
To the teachers from the principal	To my doctor from your patient
To my best friend from the family pet	To Mr. Potato Head from Mrs. Potato Head
To (you decide) from (you decide)	To _____ (name of a celebrity) from your biggest fan

Ideas

_____
_____
_____
_____
_____
_____
_____

Teacher's Notes

True and False

➙ Students read a chart of numerical information and then create questions based on the chart. Students can work alone for this activity or with one or two partners.

Materials
- One copy of the activity sheet on page 120 for each student and an extra copy for each group
- A supply of pencils and blank paper
- (Optional) Calculators

Directions to Students

Read the instructions and the chart on the activity page. Be sure to look up the information required to answer the example questions. You will have five minutes to write as many true/false questions as you can. Your questions do not have to require math computations. Put the answers to your questions on the back of your paper.

Sample Questions

1. The statistics in the chart are for two basketball seasons. (false)
2. There are seven teams in the Super Seven League. (false)
3. The Shooters won $\frac{1}{3}$ of the games they played. (true)
4. Together, the two teams with the best records won more games than the rest of the league put together. (false)
5. No team won more than 80% of all its games. (true)
6. The Bounders' opponents scored twice as many points as they did. (true)
7. The Dribblers show the greatest difference in the entire league between their points scored and points scored by their opponents. (false)

One Step Further

If time allows, ask students to exchange papers and try to answer each other's questions. Do both the author and the solver agree on the answers? Did any students write identical questions?

Name _____ Date _____

True and False

Use the chart below to write your own true and false questions. Brainstorm to create a list of questions that requires the reader to carefully read all the information in the chart.

2004 Basketball Statistics for the Super Seven League				
Team	Wins	Losses	Season totals	
			Points: team	Points: opponents
Dribblers	24	6	2880	2042
Hoopers	21	9	2550	2110
Pacers	19	11	2460	2220
Guards	12	18	2008	2560
Shooters	10	20	1668	2440
Bounders	8	22	1580	3160

Examples:

The Dribblers won twice as many games as the Guards. (true)

The Pacers' opponents scored 220 points less than they did for the entire season. (false)

Now write your own questions here. Write the answers on the back of this page.

1.
2.
3.
4.
5.
6.
7.
8.

Teacher's Notes

5 minutes

Insensitivity

➥ Students think analytically as they consider the effects of losing one of their five senses. This activity is best done individually.

Materials

- One copy of the activity sheet (half of page 122) for each student
- A supply of pencils and blank paper

Directions to Students

Which of your five senses do you think is the most important? Keep that question in mind as you select from the list of topics on your sheet. You will have five minutes to write one paragraph about at least one of the topics.

Sample Solutions: Winter lost its zing when I lost my sense of touch. My cheeks turn rosy, but I can't feel the cold air. I can't stay out long because I don't know when I'm too cold. I have to be careful to dress warmly and keep gloves on so that I don't injure my hands. Not only am I unable to feel the cold, I can't tell when my hands or feet are wet. I can't skate or play hockey because I can't feel it if I'm hurt.

Sensitivity

➥ Students further consider the value of their senses. Individual brainstorming or small groups of two or three students is appropriate for this activity. Notify students at time intervals so they can complete writing answers for all five senses.

Directions to Students

Read the instructions on your activity page. After you brainstorm the questions as a group, write your personal answers on your page. You will have five minutes to work.

Sample Solutions:

sight: seeing faces of those I love; seeing obstacles when I'm walking
hearing: ability to communicate with others; hearing television and music
touch: ability to keyboard; soft fur of my pet
smell: smelling something dangerous protects us; enjoy smelling flowers, food
taste: enjoy variety of foods; chocolate

Name _____ Date _____

Insensitivity

Imagine that you have lost one of your senses. You will have five minutes to write a one-paragraph description of one of the occasions below. Use a separate piece of paper.

- eating a chocolate ice cream cone without the sense of taste
- a traffic jam without the sense of hearing
- being outside on a cold winter day without the sense of touch
- a hot pizza without the senses of smell or taste
- Fourth of July fireworks without the sense of sight
- a kitten without the sense of touch

Sensitivity

Your five senses are listed below. You will have five minutes to brainstorm reasons why each sense is **important** or **enjoyable** to you. Write at least two personal reasons on the lines that follow each sense. Be specific. For example, under sight you might write, "looking out for traffic when crossing the street" and "watching a sunset." Be mindful of the time so you can complete answers for all five senses.

Sight	Smell
1. _____	1. _____
2. _____	2. _____
Hearing	Taste
1. _____	1. _____
2. _____	2. _____
Touch	
1. _____	
2. _____	

Teacher's Notes

Venn Diagrams

➤ Students find ways to describe Venn diagrams. They may work alone or in groups of two to four.

Materials
- One copy of the activity sheet on page 124 for each student and an extra copy for each group
- A supply of pencils and blank paper

Directions to Students
Read the instructions, and look carefully at the example of the Venn diagram on your sheet. Be sure you understand the labels on the diagram before you begin this activity. You will have five minutes to think of possible labels for the new diagrams. Write your labels in the spaces provided.

Sample Solutions:
1. A. all foods

    B. vegetables

    C. green vegetables

    D. all breads

    E. whole-wheat breads

2. F. all words

    G. nouns

    H. verbs

    I. proper nouns

    J. words that can be used as either nouns or verbs

Venn Diagrams

You may remember that Venn diagrams show how various sets are related to each other. Look at the example and the labels for each set, listed at the right.

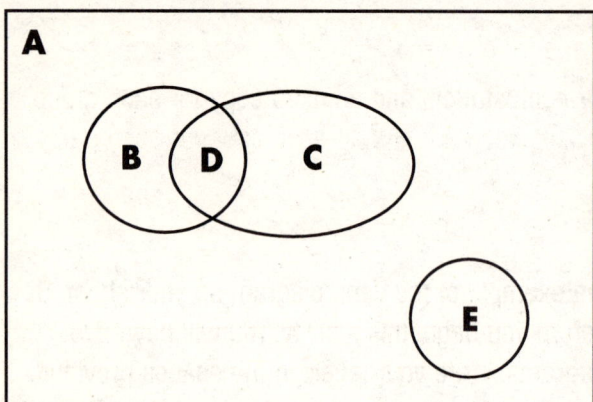

A. All names

B. Girls' names

C. Boys' names

D. names that may be used by either boys or girls

E. names of trees

You will have five minutes to brainstorm labels for these Venn diagrams.

1.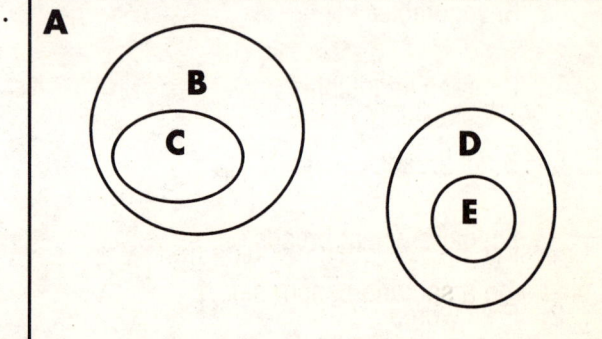

A. _____
B. _____
C. _____
D. _____
E. _____

F. _____
G. _____
H. _____
I. _____
J. _____

2.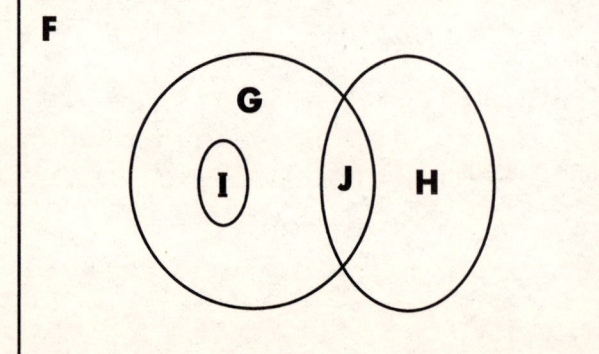

Teacher's Notes

Even Odds

➥ Students explore probability and what makes an event "fair" or "unfair." You may wish to have students work independently for this activity or in groups of two to four.

Materials

✏ One copy of the activity sheet on page 126 for each student and an extra copy for each group

✏ A supply of pencils and blank paper

Directions to Students

Read the explanation of even odds on the activity sheet. Then you will have five minutes to follow the instructions. You will list events in which two outcomes are equally likely. Also decide how the outcome of each event could be altered to make one outcome more likely than the other. Be sure to clearly explain why your change affects the odds.

Sample Solutions:

Event	Alteration
1. Choosing the right answer when guessing on a true/false quiz	Require student to correct false statements. This means it is harder to earn credit on a "false" item.
2. Choosing the salt when reaching for one shaker in a salt and pepper set	Fill both shakers with salt. Then the odds are 100% that salt will be chosen. Or, fill both with pepper; then the odds change to 0%.
3. Choosing the correct button in an elevator, either "up" or "down," when uncertain of the location of your destination	Get directions from someone in advance about which is the floor of your destination.
4. Choosing the winning football team	Assuming the teams are evenly matched, the odds could be changed if key players are out with injuries, or if certain players decide to "fix" the game.

Name _____   Date _____

Even Odds

You may already know that the odds of many events are even. That is, the chances of two events happening are sometimes equal. For example, the odds of rolling a number greater than 3 on a standard die are fifty-fifty, because there are three numbers that are 3 or below and 3 numbers greater than 3 on the die. But what would make those odds *not* even? The odds could be changed by altering the die, perhaps by weighting it so it is more likely to land in a certain position or by changing one of the numbers on the die.

You will have five minutes to think of more events in which the odds are even and then think of ways that those odds could be changed. Write your answers in the chart below.

Events with even (50-50) odds	Ways to alter the odds
1.	
2.	
3.	
4.	
5.	
6.	
7.	

Teacher's Notes

5 minutes

35

Good News/Bad News

➻ Students consider different perspectives on events as they brainstorm possible outcomes.

Materials

✎ One copy of the activity sheet on page 128 for each student and an extra copy for each group

✎ A supply of pencils and blank paper

Directions to Students

You will brainstorm to find what might be bad in a seemingly good situation. You are to think of three answers for each situation. Try to make the three answers as different as possible from each other. It's okay if some of your answers are humorous!

Sample Solutions:

1. No one believes you.
   The device has been stolen.
   You have to test it and you aren't sure it will bring you back to the present.

2. You are afraid of heights.
   You will have to leave your friends and family behind.
   You won't be able to return to Earth because the return journey is longer than your life span.

3. Someone in your family died.
   You will have to pay 75% of it in taxes.
   All your friends expect you to buy things for them.

4. You love school!
   You are a high school senior, and now you won't be able to earn enough credits for graduation.
   You won't get to eat the yummy school lunches for another month.

5. There is smoke coming out of your CPU.
   Your computer is so fast that you've already surfed the entire World Wide Web and now there's nothing left to do.
   When you're playing online chess games, you keep showing your next move before your opponent makes one.

Good News/Bad News

Complete each one of these statements with three different answers.

1. The good news is you have just invented a time-travel device. But the bad news is—

   _____
   _____
   _____

2. The good news is you've just been chosen to be the first person to live on Mars. The bad news is—

   _____
   _____
   _____

3. The good news is you've just inherited a million dollars. The bad news is—

   _____

4. The good news is that your summer vacation has just been extended for another month. The bad news is—

   _____

5. The good news is, your computer operates at a faster speed than anyone else's. You can surf the internet at a record pace. The bad news is—

   _____
   _____
   _____